The Psychology of the Asian Consumer

Why is it important to conduct research on the psychology of the Asian consumer? What research themes have already emerged? What are the relevant theories and practical applications based on this research?

These are some of the questions and issues addressed in this unique book. *The Psychology of the Asian Consumer* highlights how consumer psychology can contribute to an understanding of Asian consumer behavior and is especially timely in light of today's global economy and its focus on the Pacific Rim.

Chapters are organized around the key concepts of theory and culture and include numerous case studies and practical applications. The book focuses on research summaries that provide readers with important, need-to-know information.

The Psychology of the Asian Consumer has three distinct audiences:
(1) consumer researchers focused on developing cross-cultural consumer psychology models as well as examining insight into Asian consumer groups;
(2) course adoptions in marketing departments—consumer behavior, international marketing, and Asian business; and
(3) consumer-insight practitioners in research, consulting, and communication firms who are interested in the latest academic findings on the booming Asian market.

About the Editors

Bernd Schmitt is the Robert D. Calkins Professor of International Business at Columbia Business School. During the completion of this book he lived in Singapore, where he was the inaugural executive director of the new Institute on Asian Consumer Insight and is also Nanyang Visiting Professor at Nanyang Technological University. Dr. Schmitt is widely published and has been active as a researcher, professor, and consultant in Asia for more than twenty years.

Leonard Lee is an associate professor of marketing at the National University of Singapore Business School and was previously an associate professor at Columbia Business School. His research focuses on investigating why and how consumers shop in real-world environments, and how experiential and environmental factors affect their shopping behavior. He is also interested in understanding how emotional and cognitive factors influence consumer judgments and decision-making. His research has been published in major academic journals and featured in popular media such as the New York Times, Financial Times, and the Wall Street Journal.

The Psychology of the Asian Consumer

SCP
SOCIETY FOR
CONSUMER
PSYCHOLOGY

Edited by
Bernd Schmitt and Leonard Lee

NEW YORK AND LONDON

First published 2015
by Routledge
711 Third Avenue, New York, NY 10017

Simultaneously published
by Routledge
2 Park Square, Milton Park, Abingdon, Oxon, OX14 4RN

Routledge is an imprint of the Taylor & Francis Group, an informa business

© 2015 Taylor & Francis

The right of the editors to be identified as the authors of the editorial material, and of the authors for their individual chapters, has been asserted in accordance with sections 77 and 78 of the Copyright, Designs and Patents Act 1988.

All rights reserved. No part of this book may be reprinted or reproduced or utilised in any form or by any electronic, mechanical, or other means, now known or hereafter invented, including photocopying and recording, or in any information storage or retrieval system, without permission in writing from the publishers.

Trademark notice: Product or corporate names may be trademarks or registered trademarks, and are used only for identification and explanation without intent to infringe.

Library of Congress Cataloging in Publication Data
The psychology of the Asian consumer / edited by Bernd Schmitt and Leonard Lee.
pages cm
"Sponsored by the Society for Consumer Psychology."
Includes bibliographical references and index.
1. Consumers—Asia. 2. Consumer behavior—Asia. 3. Asians—Psychology. 4. Marketing research—Asia. 5. Marketing—Cross-cultural studies. I. Schmitt, Bernd.
HF5415.33.A78P79 2014
658.8'342095—dc 3 2014026941

ISBN: 978-0-765-64455-8 (hbk)
ISBN: 978-0-765-64647-7 (pbk)
ISBN: 978-1-315-71907-8 (ebk)

Contents

Preface		ix
1.	Why the Asian Consumer? *Bernd Schmitt*	3
2.	Emerging Research Themes on the Asian Consumer *Leonard Lee*	9

Part I. Conceptual Models and Theories

3.	Motivated Forgetting Following Social Identity Threat *Amy N. Dalton and Li Huang*	25
4.	The Paradox of Possessions: When Having Less Can Be Merrier *Haiyang Yang, Ziv Carmon, and Ravi Dhar*	29
5.	Unintended Effects of Planning in Goal Striving: Substitution and Amplification *Leona Tam, Jelena Spanjol, and José Antonio Rosa*	33
6.	The Role of Impulsivity in Impulse Purchase Decision Making: A Cross-Cultural Comparison *Sarah Hong Xiao and Michael Nicholson*	41

Part II. Cultural Differences in Consumer Behavior

7. Cultural Identity and the Antecedents of Risk Taking: Am I Good or Am I Lucky?
   Ana Valenzuela, Peter Darke, and Donnel Briley   47

8. Toward Understanding the Interplay Between Culture and Goals
   Antonios Stamatogiannakis, Haiyang Yang, and Amitava Chattopadhyay   51

9. Not All Fakes Are Created Equal: Cultural Differences in Considering Counterfeits
   Steven Chan and Nelson Amaral   55

10. Cultural Differences in Defensive Bias in Response to Deceptive Advertising
    Andy H. Ng and Peter Darke   59

Part III. Diverse Consumer Behavior Among Asian Cultures

11. Malleable Preference: A Nation Equity Perspective
    Pavitra Jindahra and Surat Teerakapibal   65

12. Consumer Self-Connections to Global Brands in Asia
    Sunmyoung Cho   89

13. Impact of Spouses' Past Influence Patterns on Economic Decision Making: A Couple's Diary Technique Applied in Vietnamese Households
    Elfriede Penz and Erich Kirchler   97

14. Sequential Cross-Sectional Studies of Values in Singapore and the United States
    Soo Jiuan Tan, Siok Kuan Tambyah, and Lynn R. Kahle   103

Part IV. Current Practices

15. Consumers' Perspective on Mobile Phone Marketing
    *Mustika Sufiati Purwanegara, Ronny Armando Pitojo,
    and Mia Tantri Diah Indriani*   119

16. Toward a Differential Understanding of Social Media
    Usage and Participation Benefits: A Cross-Cultural
    Comparison Between Eastern and Western Users
    Werner H. Kunz and Raymond R. Liu   129

17. Shape Matters: How Logo Shapes Influence
    Consumer Reactions
    *Yuwei Jiang, Gerald J. Gorn, Maria Galli,
    and Amitava Chattopadhyay*   135

18. Analyses of Corporate Visual Identities: Reaction of
    Japanese Consumers to Global Logo Changes
    Naoko Moriyoshi and Miho Sasaki   139

19. Epilogue   151

Index   153
About the Editors and Contributors   161

Preface

Why is it important to conduct research on the psychology of the Asian consumer? What research themes have already emerged? What are the relevant theories and practical applications based on this research?

These are some of the questions and issues addressed in this unique book, which is based on a conference organized by the Society of Consumer Psychology (SCP) as part of its annual Advertising and Consumer Psychology (ACP) conference, held in partnership with the Institute on Asian Consumer Insight (ACI) which was hosted by Nanyang Technological University (NTU), in Singapore, December 19–21, 2012. While co-editing this book, Bernd Schmitt was the executive director of ACI and Leonard Lee was an ACI research fellow.

The theme of the conference was "The Asian Consumer." Attended by about a hundred academics from all over the world as well as several industry participants, the conference served as an international forum, assessing the relevance of consumer psychology models for understanding Asian consumers, and, conversely, exploring new contributions to consumer psychology based on Asian consumer insight.

The conference also offered participants a full-fledged immersion into the life of Asian consumers—similar to, though shorter than, the classic "Consumer Behavior Odyssey" that some of our colleagues undertook twenty-five years ago into the lives of the American consumer. In addition to presentations and discussions, participants took a retail tour (explaining mainstream and luxury stores and shopping malls), an Asian culture tour, and a wellness and lifestyle tour. Participants watched the spectacular "Wonder Full" laser show performed at Marina Bay Sands. We had dinner at the oldest hawker center in Singapore, Lau Pa Sat. Moreover, participants were served various Asian cuisines (Chinese, Malay, Indian, and Indonesian) throughout the conference.

The conference featured two keynote speakers. The first keynote speaker was the SCP President Professor Michel Pham, who gave an overview of the achievements and unfinished tasks of consumer psychology. In his insightful speech, he paid particular attention to research on culture. Professor Pham proposed that researchers consider new perspectives in thinking about culture and incorporate the multifaceted nature of culture into their research.

> We should be looking at culture at multiple levels. It exists at the national level. It exists at the ethnic level and at the religious level. . . . It should not just be the values that we should be looking at, but we should also be recognizing the practices of the cultural systems . . . the heroes, the rituals, and the symbols that are being used in a culture are all potential areas that would be fascinating. And that's why this conference is a very appropriate time to make advances in this area of consumer behavior.

Professor Angela Lee, the second keynote speaker at the conference, presented a comprehensive review of cross-cultural research in consumer psychology. She addressed the philosophical roots of Western and Eastern thinking and how they have affected individuals' self-concepts. Professor Lee concluded her presentation with neuropsychological evidence for cross-cultural differences in thinking and behavior.

> In the West, there is Aristotle. In the East there is Confucius. . . . Thinking styles [between cultures] are very different because of these differences in philosophy. . . . In the West, people think of themselves as very positive, and in the East people see themselves as more balanced. . . . There is neuro-evidence that people think about another person differently in the two different societies.

We have organized this book into four parts: conceptual models and theories; cultural differences in consumer behavior; diverse consumer behavior among Asian cultures; and current practices. At the beginning of the book we offer our own perspectives on Asian consumers and emerging research themes. We have also written the overviews for each of the four parts. In this book, the reader can find theoretical and applied research on consumer motiviations, decision making, values, shopping, lifestyles, social media, brand perceptions—and more.

In putting together this book, we also acknowledge the help and assistance of the ACI staff, in particular, Rachel Samuil. We also thank the Center for International Business Education and Research (CIBER) at Columbia University for providing financial assistance. A special thanks is due to Stacey Victor, who provided editorial and administrative support in completing this book. Most important, we thank all the authors who contributed their papers to this book; we greatly appreciate their time and effort.

We hope that this book will stimulate further research on the psychology of the Asian consumer.

Bernd Schmitt and Leonard Lee

1

Why the Asian Consumer?

BERND SCHMITT

Why should consumer psychologists care about the Asian consumer? There is a simple practical answer to this question. Numerous economists have identified the East Asia region as one of the major growth engines for the world economy. Consequently, if the predictions of their economic studies are accurate, consumers in this region will be a dominant force in the world economy in the twenty-first century.

The Century of the Asian Consumer

Consider the following numbers and statistics. China has grown on average 9 percent annually since 1979 when it embarked on its open door policy and began experimenting with capitalism and market forces. It has lifted over 620 million of its people out of extreme poverty, and in 2010 became the world's second-largest economy after the United States, overtaking Germany, the United Kingdom, France, and all the rest of Western Europe. Admittedly, growth in other Asian countries (e.g., India and Indonesia) has been positive as well, though not as impressive as that in China. There have been bumps and roadblocks. Nonetheless, most economists taking a long-term perspective expect the future of Asian markets to be very positive. Using historical data and economic forecasts, Danny Quay, professor of economics and international development at the London School of Economics, contends that the economic center of gravity will drift eastward, and by 2050 will have moved from the United States and Western Europe to the East, or 1.5 times the radius of the planet to a point between China and India (Quay, 2010). *Megachange:*

The World in 2050, published by *The Economist*, predicts that, by 2050, Asia will be the dominant force in the world economy.

> From a historical perspective, China's emerging status as the world's leading economy will not be a novelty. It was by far the world's largest economy until the nineteenth century (in terms of purchasing power parity) accounting for 20–30 percent of the world's output. Along with India, it dominated the world economy for nearly two millennia. . . . By 2050, these two economies will have resumed that dominance. If the forecast presented here is anywhere near right, developing Asia as a whole will by mid-century account for something close to half of the world's output. Prepare for the Asian century. (Franklin and Andrews, 2012, p. 180)

At the center of these developments is the Asian consumer. A 2011 study by the Asian Development Bank found that by 2030 an additional 3 billion Asians will enjoy living standards similar to those in Europe and the United States today. Assuming a conservative growth rate of 5.5 percent, China's per capita income (at purchasing power parity) alone would then be around USD 33,000—an increase from around USD 11,000 in 2010—and about the same as current per capita income in the European Union. As a whole, the Chinese economy would be about twice the size of the U.S. economy. Some of China's consumption figures today are already mind-boggling: with a population of 1.3 billion people, China has 900 million mobile phone users, and the number of annual car sales is higher than in any other country. Middle-class consumption is also predicted to be strong in other Asian markets. A 2010 study by the OECD (Organization for Economic Cooperation and Development) Development Center, combining household survey data with growth projections for 145 countries, shows that Asia could account for over 40 percent of global middle-class consumption.

Given these extraordinary developments, it seems of paramount importance that consumer researchers begin to understand the Asian consumer and the behavior of the rapidly rising middle class in Asia. Will emerging Asian consumers behave like Western consumers when their incomes rise? How will their values and motivations change? How will they make decisions and shop for products and brands?

But Wait, Aren't We Supposed to Develop General Theories?

For most consumer psychologists, the practical significance of Asian consumers may not be enough of a reason or justification for engaging in research on them. Many consumer psychologists view their jobs as developing and testing general theories—theories that apply to all consumers (and not any specific consumer group)—and do not need to be necessarily practically relevant.

Fortunately, there are at least three additional reasons for engaging in research on Asian consumers even if one considers the purpose of the field to be theoretical (rather than practical) and focused on consumers in general (rather than specific groups).

First, by conducting research on Asian consumers, it will be possible to put our presumably general theories and principles of consumer psychology to a test. Are those consumer-psychology models and theories, which we have frequently derived from psychological theories and tested with Western consumers, in fact generally applicable and universal? Or are they a matter of historical coincidence and constrained by specific commercial environments and cultural contexts that consumers are facing? I don't mean to raise this point in a flippant way ("Cross-cultural differences, anybody?"). Rather, the environmental and contextual worlds that Asian consumers face today may be radically different from those that we constructed in Western lab experiments and field studies. These different circumstances may affect the type, speed, and ease of processing effective responses as well as purchase behaviors that we may observe. For example, the current world in Asia is one that is complex and rapidly changing, where multicultural traditions contrast with disruptive innovation, where the world of the countryside clashes with ultramodern cityscapes, and where the familiar is undermined by global influences—in other words, a world where categories of time and place are in constant flux and where identity needs to be constantly renegotiated and reconstructed. Such an environment seems quite different from the relatively straightforward, linear, and familiar world in which Western (especially American) consumers have grown up and to which they are accustomed. As a result, the basic categories to construct commercial reality as well as the processes used to make sense of such a reality may differ to some degree between Asian and American consumers. In sum, studies of Asian consumers are likely to help us enrich, and potentially revise, existing consumer psychology models and theories.

Second, some consumer phenomena may emerge almost exclusively in Asia and others may show up there first. As a result, Asian consumer behavior may be the ideal place to develop theory and conduct empirical work about these unique or new consumer phenomena. Take China's one-child policy, a generational experiment of unprecedented proportions with currently unpredictable behavioral consequences. It may be oddly habit-forming to be an only child, growing up in a society of millions of other only children. As a result, a one-child society may be a unique testing ground for studying the relation between government policies, social norms, mental schemata, and consumer behavior. Or imagine growing up in a society (South Korea) where in one year alone 20 percent of the population engages in some sort of plastic surgery. How would that change an individual's view of beauty, body, and the self? Or consider *kawaii*—the multifaceted, linguistically complex, and widely present concept of "cuteness" that was invented in Japan and is now being exported to other Asian countries. How does *Kawaii* relate to self-construal and brand perception, and about consumer communities and celebrity influence?

Third, if we conduct cross-cultural research within Asia rather than engaging in "East–West comparisons," we may contribute to developing yet another important theoretical and methodological issue. Should all Asian consumers be considered the same (say, as "collectivists" or people with "interdependent selves") and be contrasted with "Westerners" (also lumped together as "individualists" or people with "independent selves")? Or are there key differences among Asian consumers? Are we justified, or not, in aggregating across Asian markets, countries, and cultures (and Western markets, for that matter), and randomly pick one location in Asia and the West, as we have done for many years in cross-cultural research? Or do we need to adopt a more differentiated point of view because multiple cultural dimensions may be at play in shaping consumer behavior, which may not justify such a simple scheme. By conducting intra-Asian studies and examining both the similarities and differences among Asian consumers, we could find out and determine which cultural dimensions allow for an East–West comparison and which dimensions may benefit from drawing different groupings.

To stimulate research on these topics, and many others, Leonard Lee and I organized a conference with the Society of Consumer Psychology (SCP) on the "Asian consumer" in Singapore in 2012 and coedited this book, which is based on the conference.

The Eighth Sin

In a noteworthy—and much noted—presidential address three months after our conference, SCP's outgoing president, Professor Michel Pham, laid out what he called "The Seven Sins of Consumer Psychology." According to Pham (2013), these Seven Sins are "(1) a narrow conception of the scope of consumer behavior research; (2) adoption of a narrow set of theoretical lenses; (3) adherence to a narrow epistemology of consumer research; (4) an almost exclusive emphasis on psychological *processes* as opposed to psychological *content*; (5) a strong tendency to over-generalize from finite empirical results, both as authors and as reviewers; (6) a predisposition to design studies based on methodological convenience rather than on substantive considerations; and (7) a pervasive confusion between 'theories of studies' and studies of theories."

Within the context of the study of the Asian consumer, the field as a whole has committed an "eighth sin"—of blindly neglecting the rich insights that may be gained by stepping out of a Western consumer context and considering seriously the multifaceted Asian consumer culture. I trust that, with the conference and this book, we have done penance and are ready to reconcile the mainstream thinking of consumer psychology with the practical needs and broad-based theoretical potential of research on Asian consumers.

Acknowledgment

The section "The Century of the Asian Consumer" is based, in part, on research from Bernd Schmitt's book, *The Changing Face of the Asian Consumer.*

References

Franklin, D., and Andrews, J. (Eds.). (2012). *Megachange: The World in 2050.* Hoboken, NJ: John Wiley & Sons. Published by *The Economist.*

Pham, Michel. (2003). The seven sins of consumer psychology. *Journal of Consumer Psychology,* 23(4), 411–423.

Quay, Danny. (2010). The shifting distribution of global economic activity. Working paper, London School of Economics.

2

Emerging Research Themes on the Asian Consumer

LEONARD LEE

The rise of Asia is a well-recognized economic trend. In retail, in particular, demand for consumer products in Asia has seen exponential growth as spending power and desire for a better quality of life continue to escalate (PricewaterhouseCoopers, 2013). Today, countries such as China, Malaysia, Thailand, and the Philippines are home to some of the largest malls in the world. As the world watches closely the growth of Asia (Jorgenson, 2013; Studwell, 2013), marketing scholars have been attempting to obtain a deeper understanding of the minds and hearts of Asian consumers, to understand what makes them tick and how marketers can influence their purchase and consumption decisions (Nisbett, 2004; Shavitt, Lee, and Torelli, 2008).

Building upon research on the impact of culture in consumer psychology as well as research in consumer behavior, in this chapter I highlight the emerging research themes that are of particular relevance to the Asian consumer. Two important qualifications in this attempt are noteworthy. First, rather than cultural psychology in general (Chiu and Hong, 2007), this chapter focuses on examining the influence of culture on consumer psychology, in particular that of Asian consumers. Second, this chapter identifies *emerging* research themes germane to Asian consumers, using selected empirical findings from marketing articles published in the past five years to illustrate these themes; it does not provide an exhaustive review of research in cross-cultural consumer psychology (for recent comprehensive reviews of cross-cultural consumer psychology, see Shavitt, Lee, and Johnson, 2008; Shavitt et al., 2008b); rather, it reviews recent work that lies at the intersection of cultural psychology and a number of important domains in consumer behavior such as emotions, brand attitudes, consumer values, and consumer decision making.

Theme 1: The Impact of Self-Construal on Marketing Responses

Among the various dimensions of culture that Geert Hofstede (1980), a pioneer of cross-cultural psychology, identifies in his seminal work, the distinction between *individualistic* cultures and *collectivistic* cultures is no doubt the dimension that researchers have most pervasively used to compare cultures. Whereas people in individualistic cultures (e.g., North Americans) value independence and attach higher priority to personal goals than to group goals, those in collectivistic cultures (e.g., East Asians) value interdependent connections with others and view group goals as more important than their personal goals. Correspondingly, people in individualistic cultures tend to have an *independent* self-construal, perceiving themselves as autonomous and unique, while those in collectivistic cultures have an *interdependent* self-construal, perceiving themselves as members of a larger social group (Markus and Kitayama, 1991). Further, people in more collectivistic (vs. individualistic) cultures (e.g., East Asians) tend to process information more holistically (vs. analytically), pursue more promotion-focused (vs. prevention-focused) goals, expect more changes in tasks and events in their lives, and possess greater tolerance for conflict and contradiction (Cheng et al., 2012; Ji, Nisbett, and Su, 2001; Krishna, Zhou, and Zhang, 2008; Lee, Aaker, and Gardner, 2000; Nisbett and Miyamoto, 2005; Nisbett et al., 2001; Oyserman and Lee, 2008; Peng and Nisbett, 1999; Spencer-Rodgers, Williams, and Peng, 2010).

Self-Construal and the Marketing Mix

In accordance with the four pillars of the marketing mix (product, price, promotion, place), there has been considerable work in exploring how consumers with different types of self-construal evaluate brands and products, perceive price information, negotiate marketing channels, and respond to advertising appeals in different ways (Aaker and Lee, 2001; Aaker and Williams, 1998;

Escalas and Bettman, 2005; Shavitt et al., 2008a; Shavitt, Lee, and Torelli, 2008).

With regard to brands and products, for example, recent work has shown that interdependent self-construals are more likely to enhance the perceived fit of a brand extension with its parent brand, leading to greater brand-extension acceptance (Ahluwalia, 2008). This is because these individuals, as more holistic thinkers, are able to perceive or uncover relationships between stimuli and product elements more readily (see Jain, Desai, and Mao, 2007). Conversely, when a typical brand extension fails, there is also greater brand dilution among interdependent self-construals especially when they are less motivated to process the given brand information (Ng, 2010).

Individuals with different self-construals also have different product/brand preferences due to either dispositional or situational factors. For instance, interdependent self-construals tend to prefer identity-linked products when that particular aspect of their social identity is threatened, unlike independent self-construals, who tend to shun such products in the face of identity threats (White, Argo, and Sengupta, 2012). The researchers argue that interdependent self-construals, being more connected with their social groups, can access a range of social identities to compensate for their need to belong. In the same vein, compared with independent self-construals, interdependent self-construals also regard country-of-origin connections in brands as more important than self-concept connections (Swaminathan, Page, and Gürhan-Canli, 2007).

In terms of price perception, holistic-thinking interdependent self-construals are more inclined to use price information to evaluate the quality of a product, compared to independent self-construals (Lalwani and Shavitt, 2013). This heightened sense of connectedness that interdependent self-construals perceive pertains more generally to a target and its context; based on this logic, when evaluating the price of a product, interdependent self-construals show greater use of external reference prices (e.g., prices of competing products) than internal (self-generated) reference prices (Chen, 2009).

Other than brands and prices, consumers with different types of self-construal also respond differently to different types of marketing promotions. For instance, interdependent self-construals tend to prefer donation-based promotions (where purchasing a product benefits a charitable cause) to discount-based promotions, particularly when the charities are congruent with consumers' identity (Winterich and Barone, 2011). Interdependent self-construals also do not distinguish between inclusive price promotions (e.g., deals that are available to the general public) and exclusive price promotions (e.g., invitation-only promotion events), as opposed to independent self-construals, who significantly favor exclusive deals that they associate with greater uniqueness (Barone and Roy, 2010).

Pertaining to marketing channels, when making product judgments, interdependent self-construals are more likely to rely on store reputation (often associated with social image) as a cue given their greater concern with social identity (Lee and Shavitt, 2006).

Self-Construal and Consumer Decision Making

When making consumption decisions, people with an interdependent self-construal are less likely to feel constrained by self-knowledge, are more receptive to external feedback, and are more likely to incorporate such feedback into their choices (Wu, Cutright, and Fitzsimons, 2011; see also Nguyen and Belk, 2013; Torelli, 2006). Accordingly, advertisements targeted at East Asians most commonly emphasize themes of respect for group values and harmony, while those targeted at Americans center on themes of freedom, uniqueness, and rebellion against social norms (Markus and Schwartz, 2010).

However, one potential negative implication of how collectivistic individuals (with a more interdependent self-culture) approach decision making is their disproportionate concern for the avoidance of losses (vs. the achievement of gains) and the opinion of others. Interdependent self-construals (e.g., Indians) are less motivated to express their own preference in their choices and tend to select more cautious and moderate options, compared to independent self-construals, who are inclined to choose more freely according to what they like (Briley, Morris, and Simonson, 2005; Savani,

Markus, and Conner, 2008). This motivational disparity in decision making may explain in part why Americans tend to exhibit (and report themselves to have) more consistent preferences than the Japanese; another potential reason is the lower tolerance for change and conflict among the more individualistic Americans (Wilken, Miyamoto, and Uchida, 2011).

The Role of Biculturalism

Clearly, the substantial number of defining distinctions between independent (vs. interdependent) self-construals has generated a host of implications for marketing, informing the world how Asians might think and behave differently from non-Asians. However, we are witnessing considerable growth in bicultures (i.e., individuals affiliated with two cultures) today, considering the increased number of individuals who reside and work in different countries for a substantial amount of time, people living in multicultural communities such as Hong Kong and Singapore, and increased exposure to media, products, and practices from diverse cultures (Mok and Morris, 2013).

In an influential article published in the *American Psychologist,* Hong and her colleagues (2000) argue convincingly that bicultural individuals can switch between cultural frames, activate different knowledge structures, and behave in disparate ways, depending on the cultural icons to which they are exposed (e.g., Asian Americans rely more on external attributions in a judgment task after being exposed to a picture of Confucius [which primed their Asian identity] than to a picture of the American flag).

Thus, how bicultural individuals respond to cultural cues in the environment should depend on their degree of bicultural identity integration (BII), or how coherently and cohesively they represent their two cultural identities (Mok and Morris, 2013; see also Cheng, Lee, and Benet-Martínez, 2006). Specifically, high BII individuals tend to assimilate cultural cues while low BII individuals tend to behave in contrast to cultural cues. Earlier work in marketing that pertains to bilingual individuals has also shown that activating a particular identity using language manipulation can also change how they evaluate brand names (Zhang and Schmitt, 2004) and make consumption decisions (Briley et al., 2005).

Beyond Individualism-Collectivism

Because of the popularity of the individualistic-collectivistic dichotomy, cultural psychology research has been somewhat limiting and seems to have neglected other dimensions along which culture may differ. Therefore, consumer psychologists have called for a closer examination of the impact of other Hofstede cultural dimensions in consumer behavior, including horizontal/vertical (Shavitt et al., 2006), power distance (Oyserman, 2006) and masculinity/femininity (Nelson et al., 2006). (For a discussion of these extended cultural dimensions, see Shavitt et al., 2008b.)

Theme 2: Cultural Values, Beliefs and Meanings

In their work on the "neuro-culture" interaction, Shinobu Kitayama—another pioneer of cultural psychology research—and his colleague Ayse Uskul (2011) show that engagement in cultural practices changes one's neural wiring (see also Han et al., 2013). They posit that culture is "a collective process composed of cross-generational transmitted values and associated behavioral patterns (i.e., practices)"; culture is "embrained" and requires no cognitive mediation.

Consistent with this basic philosophy, there has been increasing research devoted to examining the values, beliefs, and meanings that specific cultures embrace and the powerful influences that these fundamental cultural elements exert on consumer behavior. Rather than segmenting cultures broadly into binary categories, such work represents a more refined approach by looking at the DNA of each culture. In this section, I briefly discuss three recent projects that illustrate this research focus.

The Asian Consumer Psychology of Saving Face and Belief in Fate

"Saving face," or the desire to avoid humiliation or embarrassment in front of others, is arguably one of the core social values in Asia

(Brill, 2010). Many Asians also share the belief in fate, or fatalistic thinking, a reflection of their conviction that many outcomes in life are beyond their direct control (Heine, 2001). Recent work has shown that these cultural elements can influence how Asian consumers respond to different types of service failures, which is diametrically opposed to the response of Western consumers (Chan, Wan, and Sin, 2009). Specifically, compared to Westerners, Asians, who have a greater "concern for face" and who are more likely to engage in fatalistic thinking, express greater dissatisfaction with a social failure (e.g., a rude clerk at the front desk of a hotel) than with a nonsocial failure (e.g., an untidy room in the hotel).

The greater "concern for face" among Asians also affects how they perceive price fairness. In particular, collectivistic Chinese consumers tend to perceive a stronger sense of unfairness when they discover that the price they have paid for a product at a store is higher than the price paid by a friend (in-group) than if the lower price was paid by a stranger (out-group) (Bolton, Keh, and Alba, 2010). Consequently, such negative in-group comparisons lead Chinese consumers to experience greater shame and anger and make them less likely to repurchase at the same store. In comparison, individualistic American consumers do not differ in their price-fairness perceptions between in-group and out-group references.

The Influence of Lay Beliefs

As illustrated by the impact of fatalistic beliefs in service satisfaction discussed earlier, the different lay beliefs that different cultures possess can also lead to differences in consumer preference. For instance, Asian consumers (Chinese and Indian) primed with different cultural cues (i.e., Chinese and Indian consumers were exposed to symbols of the lotus and yin-yang, respectively), which in turn increases the accessibility of different lay theories of medicine, express greater preference for traditional Chinese medicine and Ayurvedic medicine, respectively, over Western medicine. This tendency is more pronounced when there is high (vs. low) uncertainty in the diagnosis, when the time frame for treatment is long (vs. short), and when the goal for the treatment is to find an underlying cure (vs. to alleviate symptoms) (Wang, Keh, and Bolton, 2010). Interestingly, Asian consumers perceive that, compared to these traditional medicines, Western medicine places less importance on, and creates less motivation to lead, a healthy lifestyle (e.g., eating a low-fat diet and exercising regularly)—a "boomerang effect" of Western medicine.

The Meaning of Western Brands Among Chinese Consumers

While consumers may associate different meanings and personalities with different brands, possibly as a direct response to marketers' brand positioning efforts (Aaker, 1997), specific cultures may attach their own set of symbolic meanings to foreign brands. For instance, Chinese consumers tend to conceive of Western brands in several different ways based upon historical national narratives of East–West relations: Western brands as instruments of democratization, domination, or economic progress (Dong and Tian, 2009). This rich set of depictions could be used to predict situations in which Chinese consumers would purchase Western brands rather than their own national brands.

Theme 3: How Do Asian Consumers Feel?

To date, a substantial proportion of the work in cultural consumer psychology has focused on examining the cognitive underpinnings of consumer behavior. However, there has been increasing research that delves into consumers' affective experience, in line with the broad recognition today that feelings and emotions play crucial roles in influencing consumers' judgment and decision making (Cohen, Pham, and Andrade, 2008; Lee, Amir, and Ariely, 2009; Pham, 2007). Accordingly, several recent research programs on culture and emotions have added to our understanding of not only how Asian consumers think and what they think about but also how they feel.

The Experience of Mixed Emotions Among Asian Consumers

The topic of mixed emotions has been a subject of much interest among psychologists (for a comprehensive summary, see Cohen et al., 2008). Interestingly, work that lies at the intersection of culture, marketing, and mixed emotions has elucidated the factors that determine individuals' responsiveness toward stimuli that generate mixed emotions. In particular, these researchers examine consumers' degree of comfort when exposed to mixed emotional ad appeals and how much consumers are persuaded by these advertisements.

For instance, given their greater acceptance of duality and contradictions, Asian Americans are more receptive to these mixed-emotions ads than are Anglo Americans (Williams and Aaker, 2002). More recently, Hong and Lee (2010) offer a different explanation by comparing the attitudes of European-American consumers living in the United States versus Chinese consumers living in Hong Kong toward such mixed-emotional appeals in advertising. They found that the Chinese consumers in Hong Kong responded more favorably to these ad appeals and expressed a greater intention to purchase the advertised products due to their proclivity to process information at a higher construal level and focus on the positives and pro arguments (rather than the negatives and con arguments) in the ads.

How Asian Consumers Respond to Surprise Gifts

While pleasant surprises are often welcomed and can produce joy and other positive feelings, it appears that the degree of positivity in these emotional responses may not be the same across consumers. In particular, in a cross-cultural study of consumer responses to unexpected incentives, East Asian consumers tend to express less surprise and correspondingly less pleasure when receiving an unexpected gift or incentive than Caucasians in the United States (Valenzuela, Mellers, and Strebel, 2010). Such an emotional dampening could be explained by East Asians' greater desire to maintain balance and emotional control, leading them to reassess the perceived likelihood of the outcome in order to downplay the unexpectedness of the gift or incentive. However, given that East Asians also tend to view good luck favorably, they respond more positively to the unexpected gift or incentive when it is attributed to good luck, reflecting how a persistent cultural value can change their perception and emotional response.

Asian Consumers and Impulsive Behavior

The desire for harmony, balance, and connectedness can also affect Asian consumers' propensity to engage in impulsive behavior. For example, demonstrate that compared to individuals with an independent self-construal (e.g., American Caucasians), those with an interdependent self-construal (e.g., East Asians) tend to exhibit less impulsive consumption behavior, based on data pertaining to country-level beer consumption and state-level problem alcohol consumption, as well as laboratory studies in which participants' self-construal was experimentally manipulated (Zhang and Shrum, 2009). This behavioral pattern seems to arise from the greater motivation to suppress impulsive tendencies among interdependent (vs. independent) self-construals. In addition, the presence of peer pressure increases the degree of impulsive behavior among independent self-construals (but reduces such tendencies among interdependent self-construals), because of an even stronger motivation to exercise restraint and behavioral moderation in front of others.

From Understanding Asian Consumers to Understanding Consumer Psychology

Decades of research in cultural psychology have shed light on how culture affects how individuals think, feel, and behave (Nisbett, 2004). Since the turn of the twenty-first century, we have also begun to explore how cultural factors can affect consumer behavior. Beyond examining the various roles that culture plays in determining how consumers think and behave, by viewing culture as comprising a rich and elaborate set of elements and psychological mechanisms, these cultural components also present researchers with valuable avenues for testing new theories and reevaluating existing assumptions in consumer psychology. Through focusing on the psychology of the Asian consumer in particular, the research themes that have been discussed in this chapter not only underscore the many ways to approaching the vital subject of culture in consumer psychology but also contribute to a deeper and more comprehensive understanding of the influence of culture in consumer behavior. While the growing interest in Asia has certainly spurred research in consumer psychology research, it is our firm belief that this surge presents exciting possibilities in our endeavor to better understand the hearts and minds of the Asian consumer.

References

Aaker, J.L. (1997). Dimensions of brand personality. *Journal of Marketing Research,* 34, 347–356.

Aaker, J.L., and Lee, A.Y. (2001). "I" seek pleasures and "we" avoid pains: The role of self-regulatory goals in information processing and persuasion. *Journal of Consumer Research,* 28(1), 33–49.

Aaker, J.L., and Williams, P. (1998). Empathy versus pride: The influence of emotional appeals across cultures. *Journal of Consumer Research,* 25(3), 241–261.

Ahluwalia, R. (2008). How far can a brand stretch? Understanding the role of self-construal. *Journal of Marketing Research,* 45(3), 337–350.

Barone, M.J., and Roy, T. (2010). Does exclusivity always pay off? Exclusive price promotions and consumer response. *Journal of Marketing,* 74(2), 121–132.

Bolton, L.E., Keh, H.T., and Alba, J.W. (2010). How do price fairness perceptions differ across culture? *Journal of Marketing Research,* 47(3), 564–576.

Briley, D.A., Morris, M.W., and Simonson, I. (2005). Cultural chameleons: Biculturals, conformity motives, and decision making. *Journal of Consumer Psychology,* 15(4), 351–363.

Brill, A. (2010). Saving face. *Psychology Today,* November 29. http://www.psychologytoday.com/blog/chronic-healing/201011/saving-face (accessed July 5, 2014).

Chan, H., Wan, L.C., and Sin, L.Y. (2009). The contrasting effects of culture on consumer tolerance: Interpersonal face and impersonal fate. *Journal of Consumer Research,* 36(2), 292–304.

Chen, C.Y. (2009). Who I am and how I think: The impact of self-construal on the roles of internal and external reference prices in price evaluations. *Journal of Consumer Psychology,* 19(3), 416–426.

Cheng, C.Y., Chua, R.Y., Morris, M.W., and Lee, L. (2012). Finding the right mix: How the composition of self-managing multicultural teams' cultural value orientation influences performance over time. *Journal of Organizational Behavior,* 33(3), 389–411.

Cheng, C.Y., Lee, F., and Benet-Martínez, V. (2006). Assimilation and contrast effects in cultural frame switching bicultural identity integration and valence of cultural cues. *Journal of Cross-Cultural Psychology,* 37(6), 742–760.

Chiu, C.Y., and Hong, Y.Y. (2007). Cultural processes: Basic principles. In A.W. Kruglanski and E.T. Higgins (Eds.), *Social psychology: Handbook of basic principles*, 2d ed., 785–806. New York: Guilford Press.

Cohen, J.B., Pham, M.T., and Andrade, E.B. (2008). The nature and role of affect in consumer behavior. In C.P. Haugtvedt, P.M. Herr, and F.R. Kardes (Eds.), *Handbook of consumer psychology*, 297–348. New York: Lawrence Erlbaum.

Dong, L., and Tian, K. (2009). The use of western brands in asserting Chinese national identity. *Journal of Consumer Research*, 36(3), 504–523.

Escalas, J.E., and Bettman, J.R. (2005). Self-construal, reference groups, and brand meaning. *Journal of Consumer Research*, 32(3), 378–389.

Han, S., Northoff, G., Vogeley, K., Wexler, B.E., Kitayama, S., and Varnum, M.E. (2013). A cultural neuroscience approach to the biosocial nature of the human brain. *Annual Review of Psychology*, 64, 335–359.

Heine, S.J. (2001). Self as cultural product: An examination of East Asian and North American selves. *Journal of Personality*, 69(6), 881–905.

Hofstede, G. (1980). *Culture's consequences: International differences in work-related values* (Vol. 5). Newbury Park, CA: Sage.

Hong, J., and Lee, A.Y. (2010). Feeling mixed but not torn: The moderating role of construal level in mixed emotions appeals. *Journal of Consumer Research*, 37(3), 456–472.

Hong, Y.Y., Morris, M.W., Chiu, C.Y., and Benet-Martinez, V. (2000). Multicultural minds: A dynamic constructivist approach to culture and cognition. *American Psychologist*, 55(7), 709–720.

Jain, S.P., Desai, K.K., and Mao, H. (2007). The influence of chronic and situational self-construal on categorization. *Journal of Consumer Research*, 34(1), 66–76.

Ji, L.J., Nisbett, R.E., and Su, Y. (2001). Culture, change, and prediction. *Psychological Science*, 12(6), 450–456.

Jorgenson, D.W. (2013). The rise of Asia and the new world order. *Harvard Economics Review*, April 3. http://harvardecon.org/?p=2722 (accessed July 5, 2014).

Kitayama, S., and Uskul, A.K. (2011). Culture, mind, and the brain: Current evidence and future directions. *Annual Review of Psychology*, 62, 419–449.

Krishna, A., Zhou, R., and Zhang, S. (2008). The effect of self-construal on spatial judgments. *Journal of Consumer Research*, 35(2), 337–348.

Lalwani, A.K., and Shavitt, S. (2013). You get what you pay for? Self-construal influences price-quality judgments. *Journal of Consumer Research*, 40(2), 255–267.

Lee, A.Y., Aaker, J.L., and Gardner, W.L. (2000). The pleasures and pains of distinct self-construals: The role of interdependence in regulatory focus. *Journal of Personality and Social Psychology*, 78(6), 1122–1134.

Lee, K., and Shavitt, S. (2006). The use of cues depends on goals: Store reputation affects product judgments when social identity goals are salient. *Journal of Consumer Psychology*, 16(3), 260–271.

Lee, L., Amir, O., and Ariely, D. (2009). In search of homo economics: Cognitive noise and role of emotion in preference consistency. *Journal of Consumer Research*, 36(2), 173–187.

Markus, H.R., and Kitayama, S. (1991). Culture and the self: Implications for cognition, emotion, and motivation. *Psychological Review,* 98(2), 224–253.

Markus, H.R., and Schwartz, B. (2010). Does choice mean freedom and well-being? *Journal of Consumer Research,* 37(2), 344–355.

Mok, A., and Morris, M.W. (2013). Bicultural self-defense in consumer contexts: Self-protection motives are the basis for contrast versus assimilation to cultural cues. *Journal of Consumer Psychology,* 23(2), 175–188.

Nelson, M.R., Brunel, F.F., Supphellen, M., and Manchanda, R.V. (2006). Effects of culture, gender, and moral obligations on responses to charity advertising across masculine and feminine cultures. *Journal of Consumer Psychology,* 16(1), 45–56.

Ng, S. (2010). Cultural orientation and brand dilution: Impact of motivation level and extension typicality. *Journal of Marketing Research,* 47(1), 186–198.

Nguyen, T.D.T., and Belk, R.W. (2013). Harmonization Processes and Relational Meanings in Constructing Asian Weddings. *Journal of Consumer Research,* 40(3), 518–538.

Nisbett, R.E. (2004). *The geography of thought: How Asians and Westerners think differently . . . and why.* New York: Simon & Schuster.

Nisbett, R.E., and Miyamoto, Y. (2005). The influence of culture: holistic versus analytic perception. *Trends in Cognitive Sciences,* 9(10), 467–473.

Nisbett, R.E., Peng, K., Choi, I., and Norenzayan, A. (2001). Culture and systems of thought: Holistic versus analytic cognition. *Psychological Review,* 108(2), 291–310.

Oyserman, D. (2006). High power, low power, and equality: Culture beyond individualism and collectivism. *Journal of Consumer Psychology,* 16(4), 352–356.

Oyserman, D., and Lee, S.W. (2008). Does culture influence what and how we think? Effects of priming individualism and collectivism. *Psychological Bulletin,* 134(2), 311–342.

Peng, K., and Nisbett, R.E. (1999). Culture, dialectics, and reasoning about contradiction. *American Psychologist,* 54(9), 741–754.

Pham, M.T. (2007). Emotion and rationality: A critical review and interpretation of empirical evidence. *Review of General Psychology,* 11(2), 155–178.

PricewaterhouseCoopers. (2013). 2013 outlook for the retail and consumer products sector in Asia. http://www.pwc.co.nz/retail-consumer-industry-sector/publications/2013-outlook-for-the-retail-and-consumer-products-sector-in-asia/.

Savani, K., Markus, H.R., and Conner, A.L. (2008). Let your preference be your guide? Preferences and choices are more tightly linked for North Americans than for Indians. *Journal of Personality and Social Psychology,* 95(4), 861–876.

Shavitt, S., Lalwani, A.K., Zhang, J., and Torelli, C.J. (2006). The horizontal/vertical distinction in cross-cultural consumer research. *Journal of Consumer Psychology,* 16(4), 325–342.

Shavitt, S., Lee, A., and Johnson, T.P. (2008a). Cross-cultural consumer psychology. In C.P. Haugtvedt, P.M. Herr, and F.R. Kardes (Eds.), *Handbook of consumer psychology,* 1103–1131. Mahwah, NJ: Lawrence Erlbaum.

Shavitt, S., Lee, A.Y., and Torelli, C.J. (2008b). Cross-cultural issues in consumer behavior. In Michaela Wänke (Ed.), *Social psychology of consumer behaviors,* 227–240. New York: Psychology Press.

Spencer-Rodgers, J., Williams, M.J., and Peng, K. (2010). Cultural differences in expectations of change and tolerance for contradiction: A decade of empirical research. *Personality and Social Psychology Review,* 14(3), 296–312.

Studwell, J. (2013). *How Asia works: Success and failure in the world's most dynamic region.* New York: Grove Press.

Swaminathan, V., Page, K.L., and Gürhan-Canli, Z. (2007). "My" brand or "our" brand: The effects of brand relationship dimensions and self-construal on brand evaluations. *Journal of Consumer Research,* 34(2), 248–259.

Torelli, C.J. (2006). Individuality or conformity? The effect of independent and interdependent self-concepts on public judgments. *Journal of Consumer Psychology,* 16(3), 240–248.

Valenzuela, A., Mellers, B., and Strebel, J. (2010). Pleasurable surprises: A cross-cultural study of consumer responses to unexpected incentives. *Journal of Consumer Research,* 36(5), 792–805.

Wang, W., Keh, H.T., and Bolton, L.E. (2010). Lay theories of medicine and a healthy lifestyle. *Journal of Consumer Research,* 37(1), 80–97.

White, K., Argo, J.J., and Sengupta, J. (2012). Dissociative versus associative responses to social identity threat: The role of consumer self-construal. *Journal of Consumer Research,* 39(4), 704–719.

Wilken, B., Miyamoto, Y., and Uchida, Y. (2011). Cultural influences on preference consistency: Consistency at the individual and collective levels. *Journal of Consumer Psychology,* 21(3), 346–353.

Williams, P., and Aaker, J.L. (2002). Can mixed emotions peacefully coexist? *Journal of Consumer Research,* 28(4), 636–649.

Winterich, K., and Barone, M. (2011). Warm glow or cold, hard cash? Social identify effects on consumer choice for donation versus discount promotions. *Journal of Marketing Research,* 48(5), 855–868.

Wu, E.C., Cutright, K.M., and Fitzsimons, G.J. (2011). How asking "who am I?" affects what consumers buy: The influence of self-discovery on consumption. *Journal of Marketing Research,* 48(2), 296–307.

Zhang, S., and Schmitt, B.H. (2004). Activating sound and meaning: the role of language proficiency in bilingual consumer environments. *Journal of Consumer Research,* 31(1), 220–228.

Zhang, Y., and Shrum, L.J. (2009). The influence of self-construal on impulsive consumption. *Journal of Consumer Research,* 35(5), 838–850.

Part I

Conceptual Models and Theories

The research projects in this section examine a range of conceptual models and theories of consumer psychology. Although the topics in these projects are not related to Asian consumers per se and do not directly examine Asian consumers (although the participants in the studies may be Asian), the models and frameworks provided are nonetheless highly relevant to the issues covered in this book.

In Chapter 3, Amy Dalton and Li Huang offer a theoretical framework of motivated forgetting. They examine the phenomenon in the context of social-identity–linked promotions. Social identities, based on gender, race, nationality, or even university affiliation (as in this chapter), are highly salient—and ever-changing—in the culturally diverse societies in Asia. The framework that the authors employed can help predict how Asian consumers might cope with such identity-threatening situations.

Haiyang Yang, Ziv Carmon, and Ravi Dhar, in Chapter 4, examine the paradox that owning less may be more satisfying than owning more. They contribute to theory by explaining the impact of contrasting possessions on comparison standards to assess satisfaction. As Asia is growing, and as the Asian middle class acquires more and more possessions, the theoretical model in this chapter proposes that these middle-class Asians will not necessarily be more satisfied and happier.

Leona Tam, Jelena Spanjol, and José Antonio Rosa use "regulatory fit theory" in Chapter 5 to examine the start of goal striving (e.g., not to eat unhealthy snacks). They show that planning can either delay or amplify goal-directed behavior, depending on whether individuals operate under promotion or prevention focus. The study sheds light on what policy makers and governments could do to get consumers to adopt healthy lifestyle practices. The chapter also suggests what to do if the objective is to lower—or reinforce—the high saving rates currently prevalent in many Asian countries.

Finally, in Chapter 6, Sarah Hong Xiao and Michael Nicholson examine the topic of impulsivity in decisions. The topic of deliberate versus impulsive choices has a long tradition in consumer research. It is also of key importance in Asia as the consumer society further develops and offers more and more choice as well as more and more shopping outlets and media (e.g., stores, e-commerce, m-commerce) that may tempt the consumer to engage in impulsive purchases.

In sum, the theories and frameworks featured in this section are important and may be highly beneficial for conducting future research with Asian consumers in contexts that relate to their specific social and cultural circumstances.

3

Motivated Forgetting Following Social Identity Threat

AMY N. DALTON AND LI HUANG

Sigmund Freud's (1915) notion of memory repression, or motivated forgetting, suggests that people cope with unwanted memories by burying them deep in the mind, where they can lie dormant for weeks, years, or even a lifetime. Although Freud's theory has intrigued the world and stimulated fascinating research, it also has been fraught with controversy and empirical challenges. We draw on research on social identity and threat-induced coping to examine motivated forgetting in the context of memory for social identity–linked advertising.

Part of the difficulty in demonstrating motivated forgetting lies in isolating it. Memories that people are motivated to forget are often threat-provoking memories that they neglect to encode in the first place, so forgetting can be attributed to encoding processes rather than retrieval processes (Sedikides, Green, and Pinter, 2004). In contrast, consider cases where an intervening event makes otherwise neutral or positive memories difficult to confront. The death of a loved one, for example, makes retrieving fond memories of that person painful. Such contexts allow for a clean test of motivated forgetting because the threat is separated from the learned content. A similar separation can be achieved in a social identity threat paradigm that presents relatively neutral identity-linked content, facilitates its encoding, and then introduces social identity threat to motivate its forgetting.

The identity-linked content we use is identity-linked sales promotions, which target consumers based on an aspect of social identity, like gender, race, or nationality. Identity-linking occurs when firms strategically offer deals like "10 percent discount for senior citizens" or "Ladies receive 1 free drink." Because our participant population consists of Hong Kong University of Science and Technology (HKUST) students, our experiments used sales promotions offering 10 percent discounts to HKUST students. To facilitate encoding of the identity-linked promotions, we first prime students' university identity and then present the identity-linked promotions (mixed in with identity-neutral promotions). After viewing the promotions, participants are exposed to a social identity threat, a fictitious news article indicating that HKUST is underperforming relative to other local universities. After the threat, we measure memory for the identity-linked promotions in a standard old-new recognition task that presents the 20 old promotions along with 20 new ones (some identity-linked and some identity-neutral).

Using this basic framework, we test the hypothesis that even relatively neutral content can be forgotten if the content is identity-related, the identity to which that content relates is subject to threat, and consumers are motivated to protect against threat. We propose that the motivation to protect against threat depends on consumers' sense of connection to the threatened social identity, with high identifiers being more motivated to protect against threat and therefore more likely to forget identity-linked content when threatened.

Study 1 shows that priming a social identity has a positive effect on memory for identity-linked promotions. If, however, the primed identity is threatened, then the effect is reversed (i.e., consumers forget the promotions). As predicted, this effect is moderated by strength of identification, with high identifiers exhibiting better memory for identity-linked promotions when the relevant identity is primed, but worse memory for identity-linked promotions when the primed identity is threatened.

Study 2 tests the hypothesis that identity-linked content is not forgotten; it is simply not explicitly retrieved when the identity is threatened. In support of this theorizing, measuring memory implicitly reveals good memory performance even under threat. Again, this effect is moderated by strength of identification, with high identifiers exhibiting better implicit memory for the promotions under threat.

Study 3 tests the hypothesis that mitigating the threat via an identity affirmation task restores memory for otherwise forgotten identity-linked promotions. Moreover, this study shows that affirming the university identity restores memory for identity-linked promotions, but affirming aspects of self-identity or other social identities does not have this effect. Again, the results are moderated by strength of identification, with high identifiers exhibiting better memory for identity-linked promotions when the threatened aspect of identity has been affirmed, but worse memory for identity-linked promotions in the absence of identity affirmation.

This research documents an elusive memory phenomenon, motivated forgetting, and offers a theoretical framework that predicts situations in which it is likely to occur, what memories are forgotten, and who is motivated to forget. This study also contributes to research on identity-linked marketing. With mass marketing on the decline, firms increasingly rely upon targeted marketing tactics like identity-linking, but despite its widespread use, the efficacy of identity-linking remains unclear. By examining motivated forgetting in the context of identity-linked promotions, we hope not only to advance theory about motivated forgetting but also to address factors that cause consumers to remember or forget identity-linked promotions.

References

Freud, S. (1915). Repression. In James Strachey (Ed.), *The standard edition of the complete psychological works of Sigmund Freud,* Vol. 14 *(1914–1916): On the history of the psycho-analytic movement, papers on metapsychology and other works,* 141–158. London: Hogarth Press and the Institute of Psycho-analysis.

Sedikides, C., Green, J.D., and Pinter, B.T. (2004). Self-protective memory. In D.R. Beike, J.M. Lampinen, and D.A. Behrend (Eds.), *Memory and the self,* 161–179. Philadelphia: Psychology Press.

4

The Paradox of Possessions
When Having Less Can Be Merrier

HAIYANG YANG, ZIV CARMON, AND RAVI DHAR

A widespread belief among consumers is that owning more is more desirable than owning less. The yearning for additional possessions is reflected in such impressive statistics as consumers on average owning more than 19 pairs of shoes (*Time*, 2006), and average households having 2.9 TVs—more TVs than people (Nielsen, 2009). In this research, we challenge that belief, identifying a common condition in which owning more can dampen rather than boost consumer satisfaction. We also explore how cognitive style moderates this negative effect.

While prior research sheds important light on how judgments and choices are affected by options viewed jointly or in isolation (for discussion, see, e.g., Bazerman, Loewenstein, and White, 1992; Brenner, Rottenstreich, and Sood, 1999; Hsee and Leclerc, 1998; Nowlis and Simonson, 1997; see also Yang and Carmon, 2010), the effect of owning multiple goods on consumer satisfaction is not well understood. The current research advances the notion of contrasting possessions—goods that fulfill similar consumption functions with each good perceived as better than the other on important dimensions. Ownership experience makes the differences between the attributes (e.g., one TV has built-in Wi-Fi and web-surfing capability; the other TV, 3D graphics and intelligent energy-saving functionality) and attribute values (e.g., one TV has a larger screen but inferior sound quality than the other) of the goods become salient. This induces an upward shift of the comparison standard for assessing satisfaction, making each good appear deficient. Thus, compared with owning just one good, where a comparison standard naturally present in consumers' mind is applied to assess satisfaction, owning multiple goods can, ironically, be less satisfying.

While owning contrasting possessions can cause comparison standards to shift upward, the extent to which this shift occurs is likely influenced by consumers' cognitive style—how they perceive, process, and respond to stimuli. One important individual difference in cognitive style is the extent to which people rely on external contextual information versus internal standards in evaluations (also referred to as field dependence Witkin, Goodenough, and Oltman, 1979) and this individual difference has been shown to vary across cultures (Kitayama et al., 2003). In our research context, consumers with a cognitive style of relying more on external contextual information are likely to be more affected by owning multiple contrasting possessions, as the differences between the possessions are likely to alter these consumers' comparison standards more and hence affect their satisfaction more.

We tested our propositions in the lab and field. In Study 1, participants were randomly assigned one of three possession sets (SetTV1, SetTV1&2, and SetTV1&3) and asked to imagine that they owned the TV(s) for similar entertainment purposes. SetTV1&2 are contrasting possessions—TV1 had both better and worse attributes than TV2. SetTV1&3 did not—TV1 dominated TV3 on all dimensions. Although a pretest established that participants strongly preferred SetTV1&2 over the alternatives in a choice task, those who had this set were significantly less satisfied than those who had SetTV1 or SetTV1&3. That owning SetTV1&3 was more satisfying than owning the superior SetTV1&2 illustrates the detrimental impact of contrasting possessions, as TV3 was, by design, objectively inferior to TV2. Further, as an indirect measure of the comparison standard used to assess satisfaction, participants were asked rate the extent to which they thought their TV(s) deviated from the ideal TV that they had in mind.

As predicted, participants with SetTV1&2 were less satisfied than those who had SetTV1. This negative effect of owning more disappeared when the contrasting attributes were removed by downgrading the attributes of one of the TVs (downgrading from

TV2 to TV3). This suggests that the contrasting attributes were a source of the lowered satisfaction and that the negative effect of owning more could not be accounted for by a naive averaging mechanism—participants simply averaged their satisfaction with each TV when assessing their overall satisfaction with two TVs. If averaging were driving the effect, those who with an inferior set of two TVs (SetTV1&3) should have been less satisfied than those who with the superior set (SetTV1&2). Finally, the changes in participants' comparison standards mediated the differences in satisfaction.

Study 2 investigated the negative impact of owning more in the field. Consumers took home either multiple framed pictures with contrasting attributes or just one. After owning the product(s) for a few days, they responded to measures similar to those in Study 1. They were also asked to describe the attributes of the ideal framed photo that they had in mind, which served as another measure of changes in the comparison standard. Although a pretest revealed that owning more was clearly preferred in a choice task, participants who owned more were significantly less satisfied. Further, compared to participants who had one good, those who owned multiple goods described significantly more product attributes on the ideal-product measure and believed that their goods deviated from the ideal product that they had in mind significantly more. These changes in comparison standards mediated the effect of owning more on satisfaction.

Study 3 examined whether dispositional differences in cognitive style moderate the negative effect of owning more. Two possession sets (SetWatch1 and SetWatch1&2) were utilized. SetWatch1 consisted of a single good, Watch 1. SetWatch1&2 included two contrasting possessions—Watch 1 had both superior and inferior attributes versus Watch 2. Cognitive style was measured via a procedure adapted from Kitayama et al. (2003). The rest of the procedure was identical to that of Study 1. Although a pretest revealed that owning more was clearly preferred in a choice task, owning SetWatch1&2 was less satisfying than owning SetWatch1, and changes in comparison standards mediated this negative effect. Consistent with the mechanism that we propose, consumers with a cognitive style of chronically relying more on external contextual information were more affected by owning SetWatch1&2.

In sum, our findings show that, contrary to popular belief, owning more can, in fact, be less satisfying. Cognitive style, which can vary across cultures, moderates this negative effect. We contribute to theory by advancing the notion of contrasting possessions and explicating their impact on comparison standards used to assess satisfaction. Our research also yields managerial insights for promotion endeavors (e.g., avoid bundling products with contrasting attributes) and marketing strategies (e.g., position products as fulfilling unique consumption functions).

References

Bazerman, M.H., Loewenstein, G.F., and White, S.B. (1992). Reversals of preference in allocation decisions: Judging an alternative vs. choosing among alternatives. *Administrative Science Quarterly,* 37, 220–240.

Brenner, L., Rottenstreich, Y., and Sood, S. (1999). Comparison, grouping, and preference. *Psychological Science,* 10 (May), 225–229.

Hsee, C.K., and Leclerc, F. (1998). Will products look more attractive when presented separately or together? *Journal of Consumer Research,* 25(2), 175–186.

Kitayama, S., Duffy, S., Kawamura, T., and Larsen, J.T. (2003). Perceiving an object and its context in different cultures: A cultural look at new look. *Psychological Science,* 14(5), 210–216.

Nielsen (2009). More than half the homes in U.S. have three or more TVs. Press release, July 20. http://blog.nielsen.com/nielsenwire/media_entertainment/more-than-half-the-homes-in-us-have-three-or-more-tvs/ (accessed August 30, 2011).

Nowlis, S.M., and Simonson, I. (1997). Attribute-task compatibility as a determinant of consumer preference reversals. *Journal of Marketing Research,* 34(5), 205–218.

Time. (2006). Time style and design poll. March 5. www.time.com/time/arts/article/0,8599,1169863,00.html (accessed August 30, 2011).

Witkin, H.A., Goodenough, D.R., and Oltman, P.K. (1979). Psychological differentiation: Current status. *Journal of Personality and Social Psychology,* 37(7), 1127–1145.

Yang, H., and Carmon, Z. (2010). Consumer decision making. In J. Sheth and N. Malhotra (Eds.), *Wiley International Encyclopedia of Marketing.* New York: Wiley.

5

Unintended Effects of Planning in Goal Striving

Substitution and Amplification

LEONA TAM, JELENA SPANJOL,
AND JOSÉ ANTONIO ROSA

Motivation and Conceptualization

When striving toward goals (e.g., lose 5 pounds, increase savings), people often run into problems getting started, staying the course, or both. Even with strong goal intentions, initiating and persisting in goal striving are problematic (Armitage and Conner, 2001). Goal intentions are translated into goal-striving behaviors via self-regulatory processes that mediate the intention-behavior relationship. Planning one's goal pursuit in an "if-then" format (e.g., if I eat lunch in the cafeteria, I will order a salad) conserves self-regulatory strength and resources (e.g., Martijn et al., 2008), enhances goal attainment (e.g., Gollwitzer and Sheeran, 2006), and is helpful in both initiating (Brandstätter, Lengfelder, and Gollwitzer, 2001; Chasteen, Park, and Schwarz, 2001) and persisting (Achtziger, Gollwitzer, and Sheeran, 2008; Bayer, Gollwitzer, and Achtziger, 2010) in goal-striving behaviors.

Because planning enhances goal attainment via self-regulatory processes, these effects might differ when individuals are operating under self-regulatory systems that serve different needs (Higgins, 1997, 2002). While two friends might share the goal of being physically fit, for example, one might be oriented toward pursuing positive outcomes such as improved health (i.e., holds a promotion orientation), while the other might seek to avoid negative outcomes such as diabetes (i.e., holds a prevention focus). Regulatory fit theory (Higgins, 2000) extends the idea of people holding a dominant approach or avoidance orientation to encompass goal pursuit means. The theory argues that when adopted goal pursuit strategies (i.e., eager or vigilant) fit the individual's self-regulatory orientation (i.e., promotion or prevention), motivational strength and goal attainment increase (Spiegel, Grant-Pillow, and Higgins, 2004).

While regulatory fit effects are typically not examined separately for promotion and prevention fit conditions, recent studies suggest that important differences may exist. In studies with Italian and Austrian taxpayers (Holler et al., 2008; Leder et al., 2010), prevention-focused participants reacted more strongly to prevention-framed (i.e., avoid) tax information than promotion-focused participants reacted to promotion-framed (i.e., approach) information. Similar results emerged in a study assessing fairness perceptions of a possible U.S. vehicle mileage tax (Krishen, Raschke, and Mejza, 2010).

Recent studies have also identified unintended negative consequences from planning on goal striving (Dalton and Spiller, 2012; Townsend and Liu, 2012). For example, when individuals plan goal pursuit while in a concrete mind-set, planning can result in lower willingness to engage in out-of-plan goal-directed means (Belyavsky Bayuk, Janiszewski, and LeBoeuf, 2010). Concrete construal is the favored processing approach of individuals who adopt a prevention focus, as opposed to the holistic or abstract processing favored by individuals who adopt a promotion focus (Avnet and Higgins, 2003; Lee, Keller, and Sternthal, 2010; Zhu and Meyers-Levy, 2007). When the information construal level fits with the regulatory orientation (i.e., concrete with prevention; abstract with promotion), the sensitivity toward ought- or ideal-based self-regulation is magnified, making it likely that promotion and prevention fit conditions will interact with planning for goal striving (Belyavsky Bayuk et al., 2010). Two distinct effects from planning under different fit conditions are proposed: substitution and amplification.

Substitution Effect

Prevention-focused consumers are motivated by obligations and tend to see an adopted goal as minimal (i.e., what is minimally necessary to not fail; Pennington and Roese, 2003). When goals are construed as minimal standards, goal-directed behaviors are initiated more quickly (Freitas et al., 2002). In the absence of planning, prevention-fit individuals should take action toward a goal sooner than individuals in a non-fit state. When asked to develop specific plans regarding when, where, and how goal striving will be enacted, however, prevention-fit individuals are expected to interpret the act of developing detailed plans as a first step in goal striving because of the concreteness with which they conceptualize plans. Planning, in other words, is seen by prevention-fit individuals as meeting a minimum standard for goal striving behavior, and they will substitute planning for actual goal striving action.

Hypothesis 1:   Planning (vs. no planning) will delay goal striving initiation for individuals operating under prevention fit (vs. promotion fit and nonfit).

Amplification Effect

Promotion-focused consumers are motivated by hopes and tend to see an adopted goal as maximal (i.e., what is maximally possible to achieve and possibly surpass the goal; Pennington and Roese, 2003). Goals are more abstract and removed from immediate behavior for promotion-focused individuals than for prevention-focused ones, as they "occupy a mental space more temporally removed from the here-and-now" (Pennington and Roese, 2003, p. 564). In the absence of planning, promotion-fit consumers should take action toward a goal later than individuals in a nonfit or prevention fit state (Freitas et al., 2002). When asked to develop specific plans, however, promotion-fit individuals see the planning as launching the quest for their expansive goals (Belyavsky Bayuk et al., 2010), and as a result are expected to amplify goal-directed behaviors, such that planned goal-directed actions involve greater intensity over a compressed time period.

Hypothesis 2: Planning (vs. no planning) will amplify goal striving persistence in individuals operating under promotion fit (vs. prevention fit and nonfit).

Methodology and Major Findings

Three studies are conducted to test the hypotheses. Two field studies in the personal finance management ($n = 172$) and healthy snacking ($n = 183$) contexts provide evidence for the hypothesized substitution (see Figures 5.1 and 5.2) and amplification (see Figure 5.3) taking place.

Figure 5.1 **Study 1: Planning, Regulatory Fit, and Intended Initiation in Personal Finance Goal Pursuit**

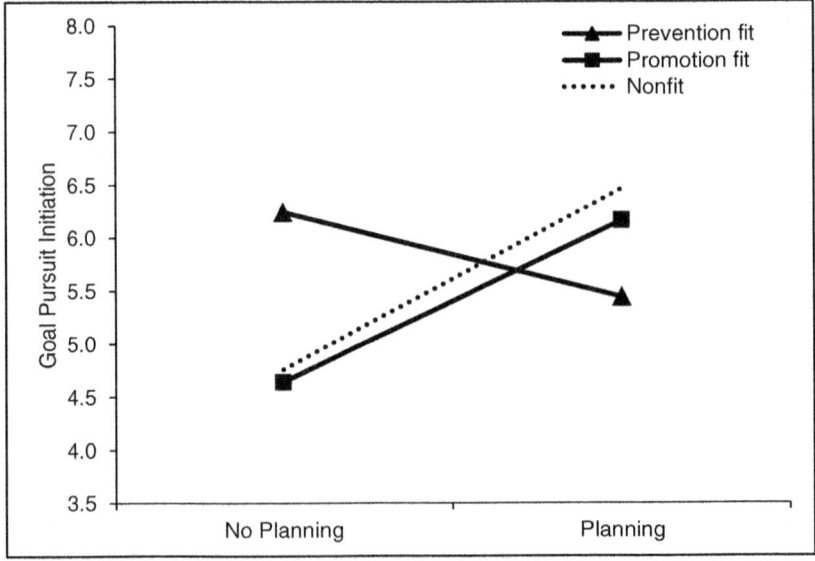

Notes: Goal pursuit initiation is measured as the number of weeks until intended goal-directed behavior. Higher initiation scores denote a faster intended start of goal-directed behaviors.

Figure 5.2 **Study 2: Planning, Regulatory Fit, and Initiation in Healthy Snacking Goal Pursuit**

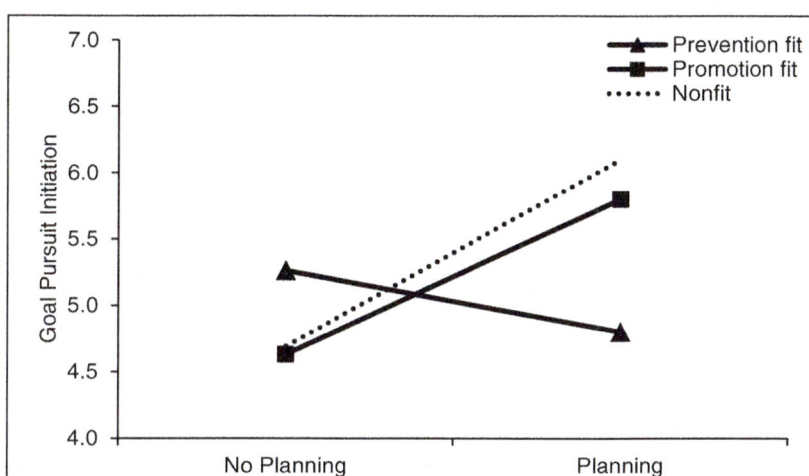

Notes: Goal pursuit initiation is measured as the number of days until the first day of healthier snacking. Higher initiation scores denote a faster start of goal pursuit.

Although planning has been identified as an effective self-regulatory tool, our research shows that planning is not universally beneficial. Across the studies, the results suggest that planning can delay as well as amplify goal-directed behaviors, depending on the self-regulatory condition of the individual. More specifically, when operating under prevention fit, individuals perceive planning as a first step in goal pursuit initiation and delay the start of actual goal-directed actions as a result. In contrast, individuals operating under promotion fit amplify goal-directed behaviors, resulting in an intense burst of goal striving. In effect, planning how, when, and where to pursue goals can backfire by delaying behavioral goal pursuit initiation (under prevention fit) and amplify goal-directed actions (under promotion fit).

Figure 5.3 **Study 2: Planning, Regulatory Fit, and Persistence Intensity in Healthy Snacking Goal Pursuit**

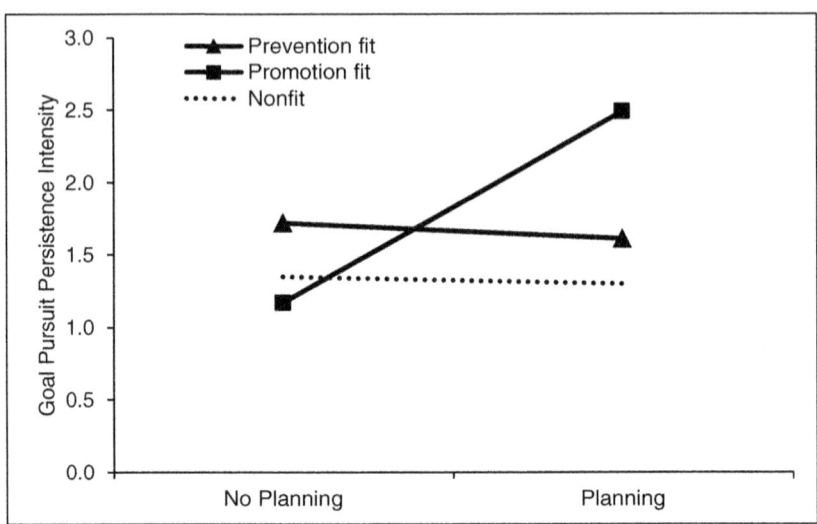

Notes: Intensity of goal pursuit persistence is measured as the number of healthy snacks consumed on the first day of healthy snacking.

References

Achtziger, A., Gollwitzer, P.M., and Sheeran, P. (2008). Implementation intentions and shielding goal striving from unwanted thoughts and feelings. *Personality and Social Psychology Bulletin,* 34, 381–393.

Armitage, C.J., and Conner, M. (2001). Efficacy of the theory of planned behaviour: A meta-analytic review. *British Journal of Social Psychology,* 40, 471–499.

Avnet, T., and Higgins, E.T. (2003). Locomotion, assessment, and regulatory fit: Value transfer from "how" to "what." *Journal of Experimental Social Psychology,* 39, 525–530.

Bayer, U.C., Gollwitzer, P.M., and Achtziger, A. (2010). Staying on track: Planned goal striving is protected from disruptive internal states. *Journal of Experimental Social Psychology,* 46, 505–514.

Belyavsky Bayuk, J., Janiszewski, C., and LeBoeuf, R.A. (2010). Letting good opportunities pass us by: Examining the role of mind-set during goal pursuit. *Journal of Consumer Research,* 37, 570–583.

Brandstätter, V., Lengfelder, A., and Gollwitzer, P.M. (2001). Implementation intentions and efficient action initiation. *Journal of Personality and Social Psychology,* 81, 946–960.

Chasteen, A.L., Park, E.C., and Schwarz, N. (2001). Implementation intentions and facilitation of prospective memory. *Psychological Science,* 12, 457–461.

Dalton, A.N., and Spiller, S.A. (2012). Too much of a good thing: The benefits of implementation intentions depend on the number of goals. *Journal of Consumer Research,* 39, 600–614.

Freitas, A.L., Liberman, N., Salovey, P., and Higgins, E.T. (2002). When to begin? Regulatory focus and initiating goal pursuit. *Personality and Social Psychology Bulletin,* 28, 121–130.

Gollwitzer, P.M., and Sheeran, P. (2006). Implementation intentions and goal achievement: A meta-analysis of effects and processes. *Advances in Experimental Social Psychology,* 38, 69–119.

Higgins, E.T. (1997). Beyond pleasure and pain. *American Psychologist,* 52, 1280–1300.

———. (2000). Making a good decision: Value from fit. *American Psychologist,* 55, 1217–1230.

———. (2002). How self-regulation creates distinct values: The case of promotion and prevention decision making. *Journal of Consumer Psychology,* 12, 177–191.

Holler, M., Hölzl, E., Kirchler, E., Leder, S., and Mannetti, L. (2008). Framing of information on the use of public finances, regulatory fit of recipients and tax compliance. *Journal of Economic Psychology,* 29, 597–611.

Krishen, A., Raschke, R., and Mejza, M. (2010). Guidelines for shaping perceptions of fairness of transportation infrastructure policies: The case of a vehicle mileage tax. *Transportation Journal,* 49, 24–38.

Leder, S., Mannetti, L., Hölzl, E., and Kirchler, E. (2010) Regulatory fit effects on perceived fiscal exchange and tax compliance. *Journal of Socio-Economics,* 39, 271–277.

Lee, A.Y., Keller, P.A., and Sternthal, B. (2010). Value from regulatory construal fit: The persuasive impact of fit between consumer goals and message concreteness. *Journal of Consumer Research,* 36, 735–747.

Martijn, C., Alberts, H. Sheeran, P., Peters, G.Y., Mikolajczak, J., and de Vries, N.K. (2008). Blocked goals, persistent action: Implementation intentions engender tenacious goal striving. *Journal of Experimental Social Psychology,* 44, 1137–1143.

Pennington, G.L., and Roese, N.J. (2003). Regulatory focus and temporal distance. *Journal of Experimental Social Psychology,* 39, 563–576.

Spiegel, S., Grant-Pillow, H., and Higgins, E.T. (2004). How regulatory fit enhances motivational strength during goal pursuit. *European Journal of Social Psychology,* 34, 39–54.

Townsend, C., and Liu, W. (2012). Is planning good for you? The differential impact of planning on self-regulation. *Journal of Consumer Research,* 39, 688–703.

Zhu, R., and Meyers-Levy, J. (2007). Exploring the cognitive mechanism that underlies regulatory focus effects. *Journal of Consumer Research,* 34, 89–96.

6

The Role of Impulsivity in Impulse Purchase Decision Making
A Cross-Cultural Comparison

SARAH HONG XIAO AND MICHAEL NICHOLSON

Impulsivity has long been established as central to the theory of impulsive consumption decision-making (e.g., Hoch and Loewenstein, 1991). Yet few studies have investigated the multidimensional constructs of impulsivity itself, the triggers affecting those constructs, and the extent to which they persist across cultural boundaries. This paper therefore examines how the constructs of impulsivity are triggered by the cultural environment, the interaction of marketing stimuli and internal emotions that lead to impulse buying (IB), across two cultures.

Previous psychological research provides ample evidence that multiple dimensions of impulsivity lead to different forms of impulsive behavior (Evenden, 1999). Surprisingly, only a few studies have identified multiple dimensions of impulsivity in consumer research. Drawing on Whiteside and Lynam (2001) and previous IB studies, we first hypothesize that four dimensions of impulsivity (i.e., urgency, premeditation, sensation-seeking and perseverance) all significantly influence IB behavior.

Second, we hypothesize that the enactment of the four dimensions and the corresponding relationship with impulsivity-behavior will be significantly influenced by cultural differences. Specifically, based on past works suggesting that consumer impulsivity is higher in individualistic countries (Kacen and Lee, 2002), we propose that collectivistic consumers will have higher premeditation and perseverance, but will have lower urgency and sensation-seeking. In contrast, individualistic consumers will have lower premeditation and perseverance, but higher sensation seeking and urgency.

Third, we hypothesize that marketing stimuli, internal emotional states, and the interaction of these two variables will moderate the impulsivity-behavior relationship. Previous studies provide evidence that both marketing stimuli and emotions affect impulse buying. We therefore propose that marketing stimuli and internal psychological states trigger activation of different dimensions of impulsivity. We further argue that marketing stimuli and emotions spontaneously influence IB.

Finally, we hypothesize that whether constructs of impulsivity influence IB depends on their constrained (or unconstrained) conditions. Drawing upon Dholakia (2000), we propose that impulsivity will be enacted by marketing stimuli and emotions in an unconstrained condition, with cognitive evaluation of behavior a less significant predictor of actual IB. In a constrained condition, impulsivity will not be enacted by triggers, but cognitive evaluation of behavior will determine whether an impulse buy occurs. However, different cultural contexts will also influence this relationship.

Two studies were conducted to test these hypotheses. Study 1 tested the first two hypotheses by conducting a large-scale survey across three countries—the UK, Lebanon, and China ($n = 831$). Cross-national invariance was generally supported. Scale items were averaged for each scale to obtain composite measures of the UPPS constructs. Results suggest that culture and all four dimensions of impulsivity all contribute to IB. Urgency, sensation-seeking and perseverance are better predictors of IB in collectivist cultures, however, while premeditation is the only dimension that predicts IB in individualistic cultures.

Study 2 examined the second two hypotheses, testing when and how impulsivity can be activated to cause IB. A 2 (constraint conditions) × 4 (constructs of impulsivity) × 4 (market stimuli) × 3 (emotional conditions) × 3 (cognitive evaluations) mixed experimental design was used, with repeated measures on the latter four factors. The experiments were carried out in two countries (UK,

$n = 200$; China, $n = 361$). After completing an impulsivity test, participants were randomly assigned to one of two constraint and unconstraint conditions, after Dholakia (2000). Participants read IB scenarios, were asked to choose between non-IB and extreme IB outcomes, and measures of cognitive evaluation, responses to marketing stimuli, and emotional responses to the environment were obtained.

Results suggest that in unconstrained conditions, consumers are more likely to manifest urgency and perseverance, and the strength of triggers (i.e., marketing stimuli and emotions) predominate in driving the impulsivity enactment. In the constrained condition, cognitive evaluation plays a more important role than impulsivity. Only urgency was weakly activated. Culture significantly contributes to IB. In both conditions, unexpectedly, the interaction of marketing stimuli and emotions played a negative and the greatest role in the IB decision. One possibility is that aggregate triggers are more likely than an individual trigger to enact an impulse buy. The negative effect of interaction indicates that the more consumers are stimulated by environmental stimuli, the less people feel positive emotions, and the more likely they are to engage in IB. However, in the constrained condition, the interaction effect has significant impact only for the British group, not the Chinese group. British consumers have much higher scores on emotion. One possible explanation is that Asian consumers are more focused on internal control, rather than environmental control, as seen in locus of control studies.

These findings suggest that constructs of impulsivity all play an important role in IB, transforming consumer actions from rationalized purchasing of products to irrational and dynamic behavior. This study makes three contributions. First, it develops a conceptual model incorporating antecedents from several levels of abstraction, focusing on the relationship between constructs of impulsivity and IB. The framework includes the constructs themselves, stimuli, and national culture. It has long been established that full understanding of individual behavior requires investigation of micro-individual and macro-cultural antecedents (e.g., Steenkamp, Hofstede, and

Wedel, 1999). We develop hypotheses regarding the main effect of specific variables on consumer impulsivity enactment and the interaction between individual differences, stimuli, and national culture. Second, we test the hypotheses in a cross-cultural context, using three countries across Europe (UK), Middle East (Lebanon), and East Asia (China); understanding of IB in the latter two are insufficient in both academic and practitioner research, despite offering great potential for the implementation of panregional marketing strategies. Third, our data set, which encompasses 1,319 consumers across three countries, provides a basis for deriving empirical generalizations regarding consumer impulsivity enactment.

References

Dholakia, U.M. (2000). Temptation and resistance: An integrated model of consumption impulse formation and enactment. *Psychology and Marketing,* 17(11), 955–982.

Evenden, J.L. (1999). Varieties of impulsivity. *Psychopharmacology (Berl),* 146(4), 348–361.

Hoch, S.J., and Loewenstein, G.F. (1991). Time-inconsistent preferences and consumer self-control. *Journal of Consumer Research,* 17(4), 429–507.

Kacen, J.J., and Lee, J.A. (2002). The influence of culture on consumer impulsive buying behavior. *Journal of Consumer Psychology,* 12(2), 163–176.

Steenkamp, J.-B.E.M., Hofstede, F., and Wedel, M. (1999). A cross-national investigation into the individual and cultural antecedents of consumer innovativeness. *Journal of Marketing,* 63(April), 55–69.

Whiteside, S.P., and Lynam, D.R. (2001). The five factor model and impulsivity: using a structural model of personality to understand impulsivity. *Personality and Individual Differences,* 30, 669–689.

Part II

Cultural Differences in Consumer Behavior

That culture plays a significant role in influencing how consumers think, feel, and behave is perhaps a well-established truism. Research comparing cross-cultural differences not only sheds light on factors that underlie variations in our cultural DNA but also illuminates the different cognitive proclivities that consumers from different cultures possess.

Broadly, cultures have been conceived of as belonging to one of two broad categories: individualistic cultures with a greater independent self-construal and collectivistic cultures with a greater interdependent self-construal. Part II comprises four chapters that examine differences between these two general cultural categories, including the United States and Canada (which represent individualistic Western cultures) and South Korea and China (which represent collectivistic East Asian cultures).

Chapters 7 and 8 examine differences in general psychological mechanisms between individuals from these two broad cultural categories.

Ana Valenzuela, Peter Darke, and Donnel Briley study how cultural differences influence individuals' propensity to take risks. Building on prior research that has shown that Westerners have an internal locus of control (believing that outcomes in life are driven by their own ability) and Easterners have an external locus of control (believing that outcomes in life are driven by situational factors), they find that self-esteem and belief in luck, respectively, drive individuals' risk preferences in these two cultures.

Antonios Stamatogiannakis, Haiyang Yang, and Amitava Chattopadhyay investigate how cultural differences affect the type of goals that individuals seek to achieve. In a series of experiments, they demonstrate that individuals from individualistic cultures are more motivated to achieve attainment goals (i.e., goals in which the desired state differs from the current state, such as decreasing one's weight from 150 pounds to 140 pounds), while individuals from more collectivistic cultures are more motivated to achieve maintenance goals (i.e., goals in which the desired and current states are the same, such as maintaining one's weight at 150 pounds or less).

Chapters 9 and 10 focus on cultural determinants of marketing-related responses to products and promotion.

Steven Chan and Nelson Amaral examine cultural differences in consumers' perception and purchase intention of different types of counterfeit products: "ghost-shift" products (unlicensed products manufactured in a licensed facility with authentic materials) and pure "replica" (copies of the original products made using inauthentic materials). They find that whereas East Asians, being more holistic thinkers, perceive the two types of counterfeit products in similar ways, Caucasians who possess a more dichotomous (black or white) belief system tend to respond more negatively to "ghost-shift" products than to pure "replicas," perceiving the former as more unethical.

Finally, Andy Ng and Peter Darke probe whether cultural differences exist in consumers' response to deceptive advertising. Their studies show that, compared to East Asians, who possess a more interdependent self-construal, European North Americans, who have a more independent self-construal, are more likely to respond to deceptive advertising negatively and employ defensive bias as a self-protection strategy, thereby perceiving a subsequent advertisement more negatively even though the ad is unrelated to the original deceptive advertisement.

Together, these findings provide new insights into how cultural differences influence individuals' cognition generally and their response to elements of the marketing mix specifically. The investigation of these differences allows us to better understand not only what constitutes Asian consumers but also how they differ from their non-Asian counterparts.

7

Cultural Identity and the Antecedents of Risk Taking

Am I Good or Am I Lucky?

ANA VALENZUELA, PETER DARKE,
AND DONNEL BRILEY

Previous literature has found that lucky experiences have a paradoxical effect on expectations of future performance (Darke and Freedman, 1997). Subjects who thought that luck was a personal, stable factor reacted to a lucky event with higher expectations for performance, while those who perceived luck as completely random had lower expectations following an initial lucky event. As a consequence, beliefs in good luck can buffer people from feelings of uncertainty and enhance risk taking. These results are quite similar to findings in the self-esteem literature concerning ego-threat (e.g., Baumeister, Heatherton, and Tice, 1993). In fact, self-esteem has been shown to predict risk taking particularly in the domain of gains (Josephs et al., 1992).

Respondents' cultural identity is expected to moderate these effects. People have implicit theories about whether behavior is driven merely by an individual's ability (internal locus of control) or by situational forces (external locus of control). Individuals' responses to success or failure are likely to differ, depending on the theory to which they subscribe (Rotter, 1966). Individuals who believe in external locus of control may be more likely to shift their expectations for future performance depending on whether they are lucky (Hong and Chiu, 1988). Research by Weisz, Rothbaum, and Blackburn (1984) indicates that East Asians tend to exhibit more external locus of control than North Americans. Moreover, Heine and Lehman

(1997) identified cultural differences in self-esteem maintenance for Japanese vs. North Americans. They found that many self-esteem–related effects, such as post-decisional dissonance, occur with North Americans but not with Japanese. As a consequence, we expect that individuals who subscribe to different implicit theories of behavior (North American vs. Chinese) will differ in their sensitivity to luck and self-esteem in risky decision making. In other words, people seem to use important dimensions of their self-concept as a buffer against different kinds of threats—in this case, the risk of losing when they take a chance on winning a large sum of money. Self-affirmation on the dimension of ability should be more effective in buffering the risk of the gamble in Western cultures while self-affirmation on personal luck should be more effective in buffering risk in Eastern cultures. Two studies investigate this proposition.

In Study 1, we use a risky decision task (e.g., Tversky and Kahneman, 1981) to analyze whether cultures differ in their sensitivity to luck and self-esteem. Subjects were asked to choose between an option with a certain outcome and another option (or prospect) with an uncertain outcome with some calculated probability. Despite differences in the level of risk involved, the expected outcomes were the same for both options. In addition, decisions pertained to either gains or losses, depending on the decision frame. For example, a positively framed decision would give subjects a choice between a sure gain of $30 and an 85 percent chance to gain $45, whereas a negatively framed decision would give subjects a choice between a sure loss of $30 and an 85 percent chance of losing $45. We ran the study using undergraduate students from both Canada and Hong Kong. Subjects completed 10 decisions (5 with a gain frame and 5 with a loss frame) presented on a computer screen. The order was randomized by subject. The alternatives in each decision differed only in terms of the amount of risk involved. When subjects chose a risky option, the final outcome was determined using a lottery procedure. There was also an initial luck manipulation: Half the subjects got $5 from the start while the other half had to participate in a lottery to earn them (although everyone won). We measured "belief in good luck" (Darke and Freedman, 1997) and "self-esteem" (Rosenberg, 1965).

Results show that neither self-esteem nor belief in luck affect behavior in loss domains for either culture. People seem to be so averse to losses that individual differences are not very important. In other words, loss aversion seems to be universally felt, though gain pursuit was not. In the gain domain, Canadian (but not Hong Kong) respondents chose the risky option more often when they rated high on self-esteem. Also in the gain domain, Hong Kong (but not Canadian) respondents chose more risky options when they had stronger beliefs in good luck. Only in Canada did the initial luck manipulation interact with self-esteem: High self-esteem subjects took more risks after winning the initial lottery. In the case of Hong Kong, the initial luck manipulation did not interact with individual's beliefs in good luck. Instead, those who believed in luck tended to take more risks regardless of the context induced by initial luck.

Study 2 replicated Study 1's design (without the initial luck manipulation) and added a between-subjects priming manipulation. U.S. Caucasian and Hong Kong undergraduate students were primed to think either about their good luck or their strong ability by describing a situation in which they were either lucky or skillful. Results showed that U.S. Caucasian respondents who were primed to think about their skill tended to choose more risky options than those who were primed about luck. Respondents who had to describe a skill-based situation believed that they were describing something more important about themselves than those who described a high luck situation. In the case of Hong Kong students, luck-belief priming did not enhance the effect of individual's belief in good luck, which again supports the idea that the belief in good luck is not as context dependent as individual self-esteem.

In sum, our results support the idea that cultures differ in how people deal with uncertainty in everyday life (Weisz et al., 1984). North Americans tend to believe in their own ability to control the situation. As a consequence, they are willing to make more risky decisions when a positive event enhances their self-esteem. In contrast, Asian cultures tend to assess the favorability of the situation and take more risk when they believe that their personal good luck will tilt the situation in their favor. In addition, the effects of self-esteem on risk taking seem to be more context dependent than the belief in good luck. Further study in risky domains that are skill based instead of luck based would shed more light on this research question.

References

Baumeister, R.F., Heatherton, T.F., and Tice, D.M. (1993). When ego threats lead to self-regulation failure: negative consequences of high self-esteem. *Journal of Personality and Social Psychology,* 64(1), 141–156.

Darke, P.R., and Freedman, J.L. (1997). The belief in good luck scale. *Journal of Research in Personality,* 31(4), 486–511.

Heine, S.J., and Lehman, D.R. (1997). Culture, dissonance, and self-affirmation. *Personality and Social Psychology Bulletin,* 23(4), 389–400.

Hong, Y.Y., and Chiu, C.Y. (1988). Sex, locus of control, and illusion of control in Hong Kong as correlates of gambling involvement. *Journal of Social Psychology,* 128(5), 667–673.

Josephs, R.A., Larrick, R.P., Steele, C.M., and Nisbett, R.E. (1992). Protecting the self from the negative consequences of risky decisions. *Journal Personality and Social Psychology,* 62(1), 26–37.

Rosenberg, M. (1965). *Society and the adolescent self-image.* Princeton: Princeton University Press.

Rotter, J.B. (1966). Generalized expectancies for internal versus external control of reinforcement. *Psychology Monographs,* 80(1), 1–28.

Tversky, A., and Kahneman, D. (1981). The framing of decisions and the psychology of choice. *Science,* 211(4481), 453–458.

Weisz, J.R., Rothbaum, F.M., and Blackburn, T.C. (1984). Standing out and standing in: The psychology of control in America and Japan. *American Psychologist,* 39(9), 955–969.

8

Toward Understanding the Interplay Between Culture and Goals

ANTONIOS STAMATOGIANNAKIS, HAIYANG YANG, AND AMITAVA CHATTOPADHYAY

From deciding which dessert to order to choosing which airline to fly so that one can accrue more "frequent flyer" points, consumer behavior is largely goal driven. Goals can be broadly dichotomized into attainment and maintenance goals: Whereas in attainment goals, the actual state differs from the desired state (e.g., decrease one's weight from 165 pounds to 164 pounds), in maintenance goals the actual and the desired states match and need to remain matched (e.g., keep one's weight at 165 pounds or less). Although extant research examined how valuation of one's labor (Brodscholl, Kober, and Higgins, 2007), satisfaction (Koo and Fishbach, 2010), and perceived difficulty (Stamatogiannakis, Chattopadhyay, and Chakravarti, 2010) differ between the two goal types, it is unclear under what circumstances consumers are more likely and more motivated to pursue each type of goal. It is also unknown whether and how consumers from different segments of the population and different cultures will behave differently toward the two goal types—an issue that affects firms' market segmentation and internationalization endeavors. The current research seeks to fill these gaps in the literature.

Cultural values are the shared, abstract ideas about what is good and desirable in a society (Williams, 1970). An important dimension of culture is whether individuals value independence vs. interdependence (Brewer and Gardner, 1996; Markus and Kitayama, 1991): Individuals from Eastern cultures tend to have interdependent self-

51

construals and uphold such values as maintaining harmony and social order. However, those from Western cultures tend to have independent self-construals and uphold such values as personal achievement and being distinct from others. Because independent cultural values often emphasize going beyond a current state (e.g., attain higher social status), they are likely to increase the appeal of attainment goals (e.g., increase one's grade point average [GPA] at school). In contrast, interdependent cultural values often emphasize maintaining the current state (e.g., maintaining the existing social order and harmony), so they are likely to increase the appeal of maintenance goals (e.g., maintain one's GPA). Thus, we posit that individuals who value independence (interdependence) tend to be more (less) motivated to pursue attainment goals.

Further, the independent and interdependent values can coexist within any person (e.g., Markus and Kitayama, 1991; Singelis, 1994), and their accessibility can be temporarily increased by contextual factors (e.g., Brewer and Gardner, 1996; Maddux et al., 2010). For such situationally activated cultural values, we expect to observe the same pattern of results—activation of independent (interdependent) values accentuates motivation for pursuing attainment (maintenance) goals, but attenuates motivation for pursuing maintenance (attainment) goals.

Finally, whereas independent cultural values emphasize undertaking actions driven by one's own will, interdependent cultural values emphasize sharing the vision of one's social group (Markus and Schwartz, 2010). Thus, framing an attainment goal as reflecting an individual's own will (hence highlighting the correspondence with independent values) is likely to boost the person's motivation to attain that goal. In contrast, framing a maintenance goal as reflecting the will of a close social group (hence highlighting the correspondence with interdependent values) is likely to increase motivation to pursue that maintenance goal. Therefore, we propose that attainment (maintenance) goals tend to be more motivating when they are framed as reflecting one's independent will (the will of one's close social group).

We tested our propositions in four studies. Study 1 had a 2 national culture (U.S. vs. China) × 2 goal type (attainment vs.

maintenance) between-participants design. Participants read a goal situation from two goal domains (exercise and finance) and indicated how motivating they found the goal of increasing (vs. maintaining) the current level (e.g., exercising more vs. maintaining the exiting level of exercising). The results show a significant interaction effect: attainment (maintenance) goals are more motivating for individuals from the United States (China).

Study 2 used a 2 (priming: independence vs. interdependence) × 2 (goal type: attainment vs. maintenance) between-participants design. First, we primed independence (interdependence; à la Brewer and Gardner, 1996). Next, participants were asked to think about their favorite charity and to indicate what amount they would like to donate to it. Subsequently, they reported their willingness to commit to donating exactly the same amount (maintenance goal) or the same amount plus 1 cent (attainment goal) for the next year. As expected, the priming × goal type interaction was significant. Willingness to commit to an attainment (maintenance) goal was higher in the independence (interdependence) priming condition.

Study 3 used a 2 × 2 mixed design with goal domain (weight and GPA goals) as the within-participants factor and goal type (attainment versus maintenance) as the between-participants factor. Moreover, we measured participants' independent vs. interdependent tendency (Singelis, 1994) and regulatory focus orientation (Higgins, 1997). Replicating previous results, the goal type × cultural tendency interaction was significant. Controlling for a potential confounding variable (regulatory focus) did not affect the significance of the pattern of findings.

In study 4, participants were assigned to a 2 × 2 between-participants design with goal framing (for self vs. for close social group) and goal type (attainment vs. maintenance). Half the participants read the attainment goal version of three goal pursuit situations (weight, GPA, and finance), and the other half read the maintenance goal version. In addition, participants in the "for self" condition were told that each goal is pursued following individual (vs. one's close social group; e.g., family) will. Consistent with our hypothesis, the framing × goal interaction was significant ($F(1,185) = 9.9$, $p < .002$) and in the predicted direction. Attainment (maintenance) goals were more motivating when they were framed as reflecting one's independent will (the will of one's close social group).

Taken together, the results of these studies provided converging support for our proposition: Cultural values interact with goal types to influence motivation for goal pursuit. This research contributes to theory and practice. Theoretically, our work is among the first to bridge two important research streams in consumer behavior: goals and cultures. Managerially, our results suggest that the two types of goals should be leveraged differently across cultures to optimize motivation for goal pursuit. Managers, for example, can engineer consumption contexts to activate respective cultural values, nudging consumers toward goals congruent with firms' marketing objectives.

References

Brewer, M.B., and Gardner, W. (1996). Who is this "we"? Levels of collective identity and self representations. *Journal of Personality and Social Psychology,* 71(1), 83–93.

Brodscholl, J.C., Kober, H., and Higgins, E.T. (2007). Strategies of self-regulation in goal attainment versus goal maintenance. *European Journal of Social Psychology,* 37(4), 628–648.

Higgins, E.T. (1997). Beyond pleasure and pain. *American Psychologist,* 52(12), 1280–1300.

Koo, M., and Fishbach, A. (2010). Climbing the goal ladder: how upcoming actions increase level of aspiration. *Journal of Personality and Social Psychology,* 99(1), 1–13.

Maddux, W.W., Yang, H., Falk, C., Adam, H., Adair, W., Endo, Y., Carmon, Z., and Heine, S.J. (2010). For whom is parting with possessions more painful? Cultural differences in the endowment effect. *Psychological Science,* 21(12), 1910–1917.

Markus, H.R., and Kitayama, S. (1991). Culture and the self: Implications for cognition, emotion, and motivation. *Psychological Review,* 98(2), 224–253.

Markus, H.R., and Schwartz, B. (2010). Does choice mean freedom and well being? *Journal of Consumer Research,* 37(2), 344–355.

Singelis, T.M. (1994). The measurement of independent and interdependent self-construals. *Personality and Social Psychology Bulletin,* 20(5), 580–591.

Stamatogiannakis, A., Chattopadhyay, A., and Chakravarti, D. (2010), Maintenance versus attainment goals: Why people think it is harder to maintain their weight than to lose a couple of kilos. In M. Campbell, J. Inman, and R. Pieters (Eds.), *Advances in Consumer Research,* 37–38, Duluth, MN: Association for Consumer Research.

Williams, R.M., Jr. (1970). *American society: A sociological interpretation.* 3d ed. New York: Knopf.

9

Not All Fakes Are Created Equal

Cultural Differences in
Considering Counterfeits

STEVEN CHAN AND NELSON AMARAL

Research in the consumption of counterfeit products has examined market size, consumer perceptions, and buyer characteristics (Nia and Zaichkowsky, 2010; Wee, Tan, and Cheok, 1995). However, little is known about how different *kinds* of counterfeits are evaluated. We contend that consumer perceptions of counterfeit products depend on the details of the item and its production. Moreover, we believe that perception and consumption of counterfeits are not universal across cultures. Differences across cultures may influence sensitivities to different types of counterfeit products. With increasing attention on the counterfeit problem around the world (*Economist,* 2012), this research intends to uncover a more dynamic understanding of counterfeit consumption.

Drawing from cultural psychology research, we propose that holistic thinking and acceptance of change are cognitive processes that influence the evaluation of counterfeit products. Prior literature has demonstrated that East Asians are relatively more holistic thinkers and accept more change and contradiction in their beliefs. In contrast, Caucasians (with European cultural background) adopt a relatively more dichotomous belief system—true or false, or, in the current context, real or fake (Morris and Peng, 1994; Peng and Nisbett, 1999).

We theorize implications of these cultural differences as applied to the everyday consumption of counterfeit products. Counterfeits are defined as illegal products made to resemble genuine goods but typically of lower quality (Lai and Zaichkowsky, 1999). A single category suffices when people are told to evaluate a product simply deemed "counterfeit" as in prior research (Wilcox, Kim, and Sen, 2009). However, one size does not fit all, especially when we know that counterfeits come in many shades in marketplaces around the world.

Consider a "ghost shift" Rolex watch, an unlicensed copy made in a licensed facility with authentic materials but on an unofficial "ghost" shift (Parloff, 2006); compare that to a "replica" made using slightly different materials in a different facility. Both are illegal copies that consumers encounter in markets. Does the "ghost shift" appear more attractive than the "replica" because it has authentic materials? Or could the "ghost shift" version be degraded because it appears more deceptive than the "replica"? How are these two items judged across cultures? We address these questions by applying cultural psychology to a more realistic marketplace of counterfeit goods.

In our first study, we presented participants with a description of one of two counterfeit sunglasses (described above as "ghost shift" and "replica"). Participants were drawn from two undergraduate populations. One group included business students from an ethnically homogeneous Midwestern school, the second from a school in New York City with a high concentration of first- or second-generation East Asian students. We divided our sample into two groups: Caucasians and East Asians. Because we contend that beliefs about change influence counterfeit evaluations, we used an incremental theorist scale as a proxy measure for tolerance of change (Levy, Stroessner, and Dweck, 1998).

Our analysis revealed a three-way interaction on product evaluations by the between-subject factor ("ghost" or "replica" sunglasses) and the two measured independent variables (culture and acceptance of change). Specifically, among the Caucasians who scored high on tolerance for change, the "replica" was preferred over the "ghost shift" sunglasses while those low on tolerance for change preferred the reverse, the "ghost shift" sunglasses. For East Asians, evaluations for the "ghost shift" and "replica" sunglasses did not differ, regardless of the measured tolerance for change. These results support our notion that, in relative terms, Caucasians were more critical of the counterfeit details across conditions, while East Asians had a more holistic view of the nongenuine items across contexts.

Our second study provides converging evidence for the role of thinking styles on evaluations of different types of counterfeit products. Here, we focus on luxury watches, given the importance of prestigious brands in most counterfeit consumption. We also extend our research beyond reductionist cultural explanations by using a wholly Caucasian sample and measuring individual differences in change beliefs. The proxy measure of change tolerance in this second study relies on a version of the Dialectical Self Scale (DSS) (Spencer-Rodgers et al., 2009), which strongly represents holistic thinking and acceptance of change (Peng and Nisbett, 1999).

In order to investigate the effects of thinking style, we investigated differences in purchase intentions between Caucasians, who were high in holistic "dialectical" thinking. An analysis of variance provided converging support for the results in the first study. Participants who were high in DSS (inclined toward holistic thinking) did not show a significant difference in preferences for the "ghost shift," "replica," or simply "counterfeit" items. However, those low in DSS showed a lower preference for the "ghost shift" item than the "replica" and "counterfeit."

In our third study, we extended our evidence from the previous two studies by attempting to manipulate participants' tolerance for change and contradiction through an established written priming task (Peng and Nisbett, 1999). This third study also relied on a broader online population (through mTurk). The first results provide converging evidence for findings from the previous two studies. More importantly, we also found that participants who were primed to rely on less holistic thinking did not differ in evaluations of either a "ghost shift" or "counterfeit" watch. These participants also reported a lower likelihood to purchase than participants who were primed to rely on greater holistic thinking. Those primed with a holistic thinking style also revealed a directionally consistent (albeit nonsignificant) difference between evaluations of the ghost shift and counterfeit products. For these participants, evaluations of the ghost shift product were higher (i.e., better) than those of the counterfeit version of the product.

Our results suggest that, indeed, not all counterfeits are created equal. Together, our findings hold important implications for how luxury brands can approach the counterfeit problem. For example, attempts to make distinctions, along moral grounds, between "better" fakes and ghost shift fakes are likely to have a marked effect in Western cultures, while they may have little impact in countries like China, where such distinctions are less relevant to the purchase of counterfeits. Furthermore, this research makes important theoretical contributions to both cultural psychology and consumer behavior. For psychology, we show promising extensions of a holistic thinking style to consumer contexts in judgments about counterfeit product information. For the field of consumer behavior, we provide a theory-driven model that accounts for the insight that not all counterfeits are equal. We conclude by reiterating that it is not simply black or white, real or fake—counterfeits have many layers, and those layers interact with a tolerance for change that is systematically different across cultures.

References

Economist. (2012). Fakes and status in China. June 23. www.economist.com/node/21557317/.
Lai, K.K.-Y., and Zaichkowsky, J.L. (1999). Brand imitation: Do the Chinese have different views? *Asia Pacific Journal of Management*, 16, 179–192.
Levy, S.R., Stroessner, S.J., and Dweck, C.S. (1998). Stereotype formation and endorsement: The role of implicit theories. *Journal of Personality and Social Psychology*, 74, 1421–1436.
Morris, M.W., and Peng, K. (1994). Culture and cause: American and Chinese attributions for social and physical events. *Journal of Personality and Social Psychology*, 67, 949–971.
Nia, A., and Zaichkowsky, J.L. (2010). Do counterfeits devalue the ownership of luxury brands? *Journal of Product and Brand Management*, 9, 485–497.
Parloff, R. (2006). Not exactly counterfeit. *Fortune*, 153, 108–112.
Peng, K.P., and Nisbett, R.E. (1999). Culture, dialectics, and reasoning about contradiction. *American Psychologist,* 54, 741–754.
Spencer-Rodgers, J., Boucher, H.C., Mori, S.C., Wang, L., and Peng, K.P. (2009). The dialectical self-concept: Contradiction, change, and holism in East Asian cultures. *Personality and Social Psychology Bulletin*, 35, 29–44.
Wee, C.-H., Tan, S.-J., and Cheok, K.-H. (1995). Non-price determinants of intention to purchase counterfeit goods. *International Marketing Review,* 12, 19–46.
Wilcox, K., Kim, H.M., and Sen, S. (2009). Why do consumers buy counterfeit luxury brands? *Journal of Marketing Research*, 46, 247–259.

10

Cultural Differences in Defensive Bias in Response to Deceptive Advertising

ANDY H. NG AND PETER DARKE

According to Gardner (1975, p. 42), deceptive advertising occurs when "an advertisement (or advertising campaign) leaves the consumer with an impression(s) and/or belief(s) different from what would normally be expected if the consumer had reasonable knowledge, and that impression(s) and/or belief(s) is factually untrue or potentially misleading." The purpose of this chapter is to examine one specific psychological consequence in response to deceptive advertising, that of defensive bias, from a cultural perspective.

If an individual has been misled by an advertisement, it is understandable that she may no longer trust the company. In fact, she may even become distrustful of marketing claims in general because she feels fooled by the deceptive advertisement. This was indeed found by Darke and Ritchie (2007). The sense of distrust induced by a deceptive advertisement negatively biases the evaluation of a product of a second-party firm that has nothing to do with the original deception. This is unfortunate because the negative effects of deceptive advertising of one company spread to other companies that may be more honest and ethical.

Cultural psychology has found that many cognitive processes and behaviors are culturally moderated. People who engage in collectivistic cultural contexts, such as Asia, tend to put a higher premium on relational concerns with close in-group members while putting a less permeable boundary between in-group and out-group members, compared with people who engage in less collectivistic cultural contexts, such as European North Americans (Markus and Kitayama, 1991). As such, it has been found that Asians exhibit less generalized trust in persons outside their interpersonal relationship networks than do European Americans (Miller and Mitamura, 2003; Yamagishi and Yamagishi, 1994). In addition, due to their collectivistic orientation, Asians (vs. European Americans) are more attuned to situational attributions of behaviors, including how social roles and obligations constrain behavior (Choi and Nisbett, 1998). Hence, the purpose of advertising (i.e., to promote sales of a product) might be relatively salient in the mind of Asians due to their chronic sensitivity to external causes of behaviors. Relatedly, collectivistic Asians (vs. European North Americans) also tend to have a more prominent interdependent self-construal but a less prominent independent self-construal (Markus and Kitayama, 1991). That is, Asians (vs. European North Americans) tend to have a self-view that is based more on interpersonal relationships, social status, and social roles (i.e., more interdependent) but less on internal qualities (i.e., less independent). Consequently, compared to European North Americans, Asians are less motivated to view themselves positively concerning their efficacy, competence, and desirable internal qualities (Heine and Hamamura, 2007).

We propose that cultural differences in generalized trust and the prominence of independent self-construal will influence the degree of defensive bias in the context of advertising. First, as generalized trust seems to be higher in the European North American (vs. Asian) context, deceptive advertising, which can be interpreted as a violation of trust, may induce negative psychological consequences to a higher degree. Second, misleading advertisements create a threat to the self-perception that the individual is an intelligent, capable consumer, and defensive bias can serve as a strategy that forestalls the possibility of being fooled again by deceptive advertising (Darke and Ritchie, 2007). As Asians are less likely to construe themselves independently (Markus and Kitayama, 1991), they may be less likely than European North Americans to employ defensive bias as a self-protection strategy. Thus, we hypothesize that deceptive advertising would have a weaker negative effect on subsequent evaluation of a product of a second-party firm among participants of Asian descent than among participants of European descent and conducted an experiment to test this hypothesis.

This experiment was conducted in Canada with 25 students of European descent and 52 students of Asian descent. First, participants read an advertising claim from a company called Depuis. Then, the presence of deception was manipulated. In the deception condition, participants read a correction notice from Depuis, admitting that its advertisement was misleading. In the control condition, participants did not receive any additional information. After the deception manipulation, participants were asked to complete some unrelated filler tasks. Following this, participants read a single-page Internet advertisement for a new desktop computer from a different advertiser and answered a few questions about their overall evaluation of the computer. At the end of the study, participants were asked to rate the degree to which they experienced self-threat.

To examine our hypothesis that culture would moderate the effect of deception on evaluation of a product of a second-party firm, analysis of variances were conducted on the evaluation of the new computer with culture (European Canadian vs. Asian Canadian) and deception (presence vs. absence) as independent variables. Results indicated a main effect of deception, $F(1, 73) = 7.35, p = .01, \eta_p^2 = .09$, qualified by an interaction effect of deception and culture, $F(1, 73) = 4.33, p = .04, \eta_p^2 = .06$. Simple main effect analyses revealed that among European-Canadian participants, those in the deception condition had a more negative attitude toward the new computer ($M = 4.65, SD = 1.83$) than those in the no-deception control condition ($M = 6.68, SD = 1.74$), $p = .01$, but the difference between deception ($M = 5.59, SD = 1.54$) and no-deception control ($M = 5.85, SD = 1.76$) conditions was not statistically significant among Asian-Canadian participants, $p = .58$. This suggests that the negative effect of deception was generalized to the evaluation of a product of a second-party firm among Canadian participants of European descent but not among Canadian participants of Asian descent, consistent with our hypothesis.

Our results highlight that consequences of deceptive advertising may differ as a function of culture. Increased understanding of the boundary conditions and moderating factors of the negative consequences of deceptive advertising has important implications. For instance, concerns about the general suspicions aroused as a consequence of corrective advertising seem less problematic among Asian consumers. From a theoretical point of view, given the independent-interdependent reasoning underlying our main hypothesis, the fact that culture moderated the effects of generalized suspicion serves as further evidence of its defensive nature.

References

Choi, I., and Nisbett, R.E. (1998). Situational salience and cultural differences in the correspondence bias and actor-observer bias. *Personality and Social Psychology Bulletin,* 24, 949–960.

Darke, P.R., and Ritchie, R.J.B. (2007). The defensive consumer: Advertising deception, defensive processing, and distrust. *Journal of Marketing Research,* 44, 114–127. doi:10.1509/jmkr.44.1.114.

Gardner, D.M. (1975). Deception in advertising: A conceptual approach. *Journal of Marketing,* 39, 40–46. doi:10.2307/1250801.

Heine, S.J., and Hamamura, T. (2007). In search of East Asian self-enhancement. *Personality and Social Psychology Review,* 11, 1–24. doi:10.1177/1088868306294587.

Markus, H.R., and Kitayama, S. (1991). Culture and the self: Implications for cognition, emotion, and motivation. *Psychological Review,* 98, 224–253. doi:10.1037/0033-295X.98.2.224.

Miller, A.S., and Mitamura, T. (2003). Are surveys on trust trustworthy? *Social Psychology Quarterly,* 66, 62–70. doi:10.2307/3090141.

Yamagishi, T., and Yamagishi, M. (1994). Trust and commitment in the United States and Japan. *Motivation and Emotion,* 18, 129–166. doi:10.1007/BF02249397.

Part III

Diverse Consumer Behavior Among Asian Cultures

Despite the substantial body of extant research in cultural psychology that focuses on examining cognitive and behavioral differences between two broad cultural categories—individualistic cultures with a greater independent self-construal (e.g., Caucasian Americans) and collectivistic cultures with a greater interdependent self-construal (e.g., East Asians), significant variations exist among the various Asian cultures in terms of people's values, beliefs, and attitudes. Hence, a more in-depth understanding of what is unique about each of these Asian cultures as well as what is common among them is essential to avoid cultural overgeneralization and consumer insensitivity.

Part III comprises four chapters that delve more deeply into the psychology of consumers in four Asian countries—from the emerging markets of Thailand and Vietnam to the more affluent countries of South Korea and Singapore. Employing a large variety of research methodologies, these chapters examine consumers' values, economic decision-making processes and their attitudes toward global brands and cultural products in Asia.

In Chapter 11, Pavitra Jindahra and Surat Teerakapibal explore how country-of-origin effects and nation equity (i.e., the amount of goodwill associated with a country) simultaneously influence consumer preference in Thailand. Through a regression analysis of consumer survey data, the authors discover that while country-of-origin matters in the products that consumers choose, nation equity enhances consumer preference for cultural goods (e.g., a TV series from a particular country) especially when the country of origin is not preferred. They also document a number of age and gender variations in their results.

Using a combination of research approaches—interviews, surveys, and experiments—in Chapter 12 Sunmyoung Cho examines consumers' connection with global brands in South Korea. She finds that Korean consumers' early meaningful self-enhancing experiences with focal brands during adolescence play a significant role in their subsequent adoration of Western global culture and cosmopolitan outlook in life.

Moving from brands and products to more general decision-making, Elfriede Penz and Erich Kirchler in Chapter 13 adopt a longitudinal diary approach, with hierarchical regression analyses to investigate how households in Vietnam make everyday economic decisions. Among the many results that they document, they find that even though Vietnamese men generally have more power and influence than their wives in household economic decisions, there is clear role segmentation between husband and wife, in contrast to what has been found in Europe. In addition, a couple's past decisions tend to positively affect their subsequent decisions without attempts to balance the relative influence between husband and wife in these situations.

More generally, in a comprehensive cross-sectional study involving a nationally representative sample of almost 5,000 survey respondents in three separate years (1996, 2001, and 2011) in Chapter 14, Soo Jiuan Tan, Siok Kuan Tambyah, and Lynn Kahle investigate temporal changes in people's values in life in Singapore, comparing these national trends with those in the United States. They discover, for instance, that whereas the perceived relative importance of security in Singapore has gained prominence over the fifteen-year period, the desire to be well-respected by others has declined in importance. In comparison, the perceived importance of both values remained largely stable in the United States from 1976 to 2007.

In sum, the specificity of these empirical results underscores the fact that although the various cultures in Asia share many similarities, each culture also possesses myriad unique qualities, rendering a "one-size-fits-all" mind-set untenable. These findings therefore call for a need to reexamine our assumptions about the characteristics of Asian cultures and for a more in-depth study of each of these cultures.

11

Malleable Preference
A Nation Equity Perspective

PAVITRA JINDAHRA AND SURAT TEERAKAPIBAL

The advance of globalization spreads national culture flows dynamically. World Bank (2003) reports that cultural and creative industries account for over 7 percent of the world's gross domestic products (GDP). According to UNESCO (2005), world imports of cultural goods increased from US$38.3 billion in 1994 to US$59.2 billion in 2002. Furthermore, this figure continues to grow at an average of 8.8 percent per year from 2002 to 2011 (UNCTAD, 2013). This reflects the vital of cultural liberty, the capability of people to live and be what they choose with adequate options to consider (UNDP, 2004), in consumer choices. Cultural liberty, hence allows consumers to adopt different lifestyles, values, and practices. This freedom not only encourages more choices but also changes the way in which consumers perceive local and foreign cultures and thus images of countries. Inevitably, consumers' purchase decisions are revised according to the dynamic flow of culture (Batra et al., 2000; Ben-Zion and Donnenfield, 1983; Shy, 2000). Nevertheless, national branding campaigns focusing on a few strengths of the country have been promoted consistently across countries (Anholt, 2007; Dinnie, 2008).

The globalization of culture has raised the fear of indigenization of foreign cultures. In fostering national identities, many governments have adopted an approach of cultural protectionism (Appadurai, 1996; Krishna, 2010; Tomlinson, 2003). For example, the French government attempts to preserve its language by replacing foreign words—such as Walkman, talk show, and prime time—with French terms. In 1995, the Canadian federal government levied taxes on all advertising revenue on foreign magazine producers. The Chinese government enforced Chinese-sounding name on brands and names of over 20,000 Western companies. Saudi Arabia adopted "modernization without Westernization," censoring all Western imports (e.g., movies, alcohol, and Internet access) (Globalization101.org, 2012). However, this worry has gone beyond Americanization, or perhaps Japanization for Koreans, or Koreanization for Thais (Appadurai, 1996). That is, foreign cultural absorption by polities at large muddies national cultural sovereignty, thereby putting into question the cultural-economic performance of the country.

In response to the indigenization of foreign cultures, South Korea has chosen to export its popular culture systematically. There emerges the convergence of taste in media consumption known as the *Korean wave,* the significant increase in the popularity of South Korean entertainment starting in the 1990s. In 2009, South Korean president Lee Myung-Bak formed a Presidential Council on Nation Branding to proactively shape and manage the South Korean image and reputation. Based on international activity, the Korean wave added approximately US$3.8 billion in revenue to the South Korean economy in 2011 (Forster, 2012). The number of foreign visitors to South Korea increased from 6.89 million in 2008 to 8.80 million in 2010 (Korea Tourism Organization, 2013). In 2010, the country experienced a 159 percent increase in music exports from the previous year (Jin, 2012). The question of how widespread the translation of popular culture is to economic prosperity remains.

Many studies have investigated national factors that influence consumer product evaluation processes. It is evident that consumers evaluate products based on their country of origin. Favorable country-of-origin perceptions are often reflected in correspondingly favorable product evaluations (Maheswaran, 1994). The country of origin affects product evaluation profoundly across product categories (Elliot and Cameron, 1994; Ettenson, 1993; Han and Terpstra, 1988; Profeta, Balling, and Roosen, 2012; Verlegh, Steenkamp, and Meulenberg, 2005). Chao (1993) posits that consumer evaluations of design and product qualities are influenced not only by price but also the country of design and the country of assembly. Notably, the traditional price-quality relationship appears to be country specific. Hong and Wyer (1989) reasoned that country-of-origin affects product evaluation while stimulating consumers to think about product attribute information more extensively. Hence, country-of-origin effect should be implemented by government entities to promote exports especially the resource-poor countries (Bilkey and Nes, 1982).

Interestingly, many studies explain that variations in country-of-origin effects on consumer preference emerge from sociodemographic characteristics. Schooler (1971) has found that females and the educated prefer foreign products more than their male and uneducated counterparts, respectively. Nonwhites, moreover, evaluate products from Africa, Latin America, and India more positively than white people. Gurhan-Canli and Maheswaran (2000) have ascertained that the vertical dimension of individualism and collectivism expounds the magnitude of the country-of-origin effect.

Despite various findings of country of origin on consumer perceptions, Agrawal and Kamakura (1999) argue that the country-of-origin cue has a limited effect on price premiums or discounts when differences in product quality are considered. This argument is further emphasized by the finding that the country of origin's image affects purchase intentions indirectly, as its influence is fully mediated by brand image when the effect of brand familiarity is controlling for (Diamantopoulos, Schelegelmich, and Palihawadana, 2011).

Studies on nation equity offer explications of both product- and non–product-related country-of-origin perceptions in influencing consumer choices. The "nation equity" is defined as "equity or goodwill associated with a country" (Mahesrawan and Chen, 2009) and may be gauged by measures such as the Anholt-GfK Roper national brand indexes (NBI) (Anholt, 2005). The NBI is the consumer perception of a country's competence—that is, consumers form positive or negative feelings toward a country based on cultural, political, historical, and economic factors. These perceptions, in turn, influence consumers' evaluations and purchase intentions of the products of the countries (Hong and Kang, 2006; Klein, Ettenson, and Morris,

1998; Mahesrawan and Chen, 2006). Consequently, the country has been used as a product cue. Pecotich and Rosenthal (2001) claim that the country cue is most effective when presented in conjunction with a strong national brand image. Countries attempt to improve and promote their identity to a wide range of audiences around the world through nation branding (Aronczyk, 2009).

Cultural liberty exposes consumers to a variety of cultural choices, such as lifestyle and value, changing how consumers view their own and foreign countries' image—the perceived nation equity. However, little is known about how the perception of nation equity has influenced consumers' decisions. This chapter examines the roles of country-of-origin as well as nation equity on consumers' cultural goods consumption. To understand consumers in the new global cultural economy, we investigate the following questions:

- What are the key roles of culture and other forms of nation equity in influencing consumer preference and decision processes? Does the country-of-origin effect exist amid cultural globalization?
- How can nation equity be translated into an economic outcome? Does the effectiveness of nation branding vary across age groups and consumer segments?

In pursuit of answers to these questions, a mixture of nested logit and mixed logit models is used to estimate consumer demand. This model addresses the preference formation based on the perception of nation equity and the country of origin as well as heterogeneity in decision processes. The model is applied to conjoint choice data on TV series of three countries (the United States, South Korea, and Thailand) among Thai consumers, along with detailed sociodemographic variables and respondents' self-reported NBIs. The data are randomly split into calibration and holdout samples. The data from the calibration sample of 333 respondents are used in the estimation. The holdout sample of 169 respondents is used for predictive validity assessment.

In addition to the presence of heterogeneity in decision processes, we found that consumer preference is not fixed and is malleable via perceptions regarding nation equity—that is, influencing consumer preferences via nation equity such as nation-branding campaigns is an effective tool for managing the cultural economy. Furthermore, these campaigns remain beneficial even in the case in which a country suffers from a negative country-of-origin effect such as in the case of South Korean TV series. However, nation equity campaigns must be carefully targeted, as their impacts differ across age and gender. Moreover, different dimensions of nation equity influence a nation differently in terms of magnitude and polarity.

Data

Data were collected in a personal interview survey during November–December 2009 in Bangkok and its vicinities as part of a study on the *Dynamic of Global Culture and Its Effects on Thailand's Culture and Society* (Nattavuthisit, Prasarnphanich, and Jindahra, 2010) initiated by Thailand's Office of the National and Social Economic Development Board. The data contain a conjoint choice experiment for TV series, NBIs, and sociodemographics of 502 respondents. The data from the calibration sample of 333 respondents are used in the estimation. The holdout sample of 169 respondents is used for predictive validity assessment. Table 11.1 presents demographic variables of respondents. Respondents are representative in terms of both gender and age.

A common orthogonal design matrix was developed using effects coding with the following attribute levels: Genre has three levels: *romantic comedy, period,* and *action.* Country-of-origin has three levels: *South Korea, Thailand,* and *the United States.* Public opinion has two levels: *positive* and *negative* public opinion. Actor comprises two levels: *favorite star* and *without favorite star.* This TV series conjoint study includes nine profile sets, each of which consists of four profiles. Table 11.2 provides summary statistics of choices made by respondents. Note that there is a preference for *romantic comedy.* In terms of the country of origin, the order of popularity, from the highest, is *the United States, Thailand,* and *South Korea. Positive reviews* and *favorite stars* contribute more shares as expected.

Table 11.1

Respondent Characteristics

Attribute	Range	%
Gender	Male	42.04
	Female	57.96
Age	< 18	22.52
	18–25	33.33
	26–35	28.23
	> 35	15.92

In evaluating nation equity, we adopt the NBI of Anholt-GfK Roper (Anholt, 2005), which measures the images of nations based on consumers' perceived national competence. This approach includes the country-of-origin product-related appeal and nonproduct appeal. In particular, the NBI gauges six dimensions of the perceived nation competency: exports, governance, culture, people, tourism, and immigration and investment. *Exports* refer to the country of origin effect plus national strength in science and technology and creative energy. *Governance* is the perceived competency and honesty of government, respect for citizens, and global behavior in the areas of international peace and security, environment protection, and world poverty reduction. *Culture* measures perceptions of a country's heritage, its contemporary culture, and its excellence in sports. *People* represent the friendliness of the citizens as well as human resource quality. *Tourism* refers to natural beauty, historic buildings and monuments, and vibrant city life and urban attractions. *Immigration and investment* gauges the ability of the country in attracting talent and capital. There are between 3 and 5 ratings questions for each dimension index, whose scale is from 1 (worst) to 7 (best). Summary statistics of national competence dimension are shown in Table 11.3.

Model

The fundamental idea of the estimating model is to capture the consumer preference structure based on perceived nation equity in addition to the country-of-origin effect. The preference struc-

Table 11.2

Summary Statistics of National Dimension Competence

Attribute	Mean	Std	Min	Max
South Korean Exports Index	4.61	1.00	1.33	7.00
South Korean Governance Index	4.17	0.97	1.00	6.20
South Korean Culture Index	4.52	0.99	1.33	6.67
South Korean People Index	4.26	1.07	1.00	7.00
South Korean Tourism Index	4.66	1.04	1.00	7.00
South Korean Immigration and Investment Index	4.24	0.93	1.00	7.00
Thai Exports Index	4.34	1.06	1.33	7.00
Thai Governance Index	3.47	1.13	1.00	6.40
Thai Culture Index	4.76	1.04	1.00	7.00
Thai People Index	5.35	1.11	1.67	7.00
Thai Tourism Index	5.46	0.99	1.75	7.00
Thai Immigration and Investment Index	4.36	1.00	1.20	7.00
U.S. Exports Index	5.40	1.12	1.00	7.00
U.S. Governance Index	4.80	1.09	1.00	7.00
U.S. Culture Index	4.70	1.05	1.33	7.00
U.S. People Index	4.61	1.13	1.00	7.00
U.S. Tourism Index	4.79	1.05	1.75	7.00
U.S. Immigration and Investment Index	5.15	1.09	1.40	7.00

Table 11.3

Summary Statistics of Variables

Attribute Range	%	Attribute Range	%
Genre		**Country of Origin**	
Romantic comedy	40.81	South Korea	28.84
Period	26.69	Thailand	33.57
Action	32.49	United States	37.59
Favorite stars		**Reviews**	
Favorite stars	60.06	Positive	66.20
No favorite stars	39.94	Negative	33.80

ture is flexible enough in reflecting that the consumer revises his preference according to his perceived nation competence or nation equity.

Relative Nation Brand Index

To incorporate the nation equity in the model, we use the relative effect of NBI rather than absolute value in benchmarking against the reference country. This approach is beneficial in preserving NBI information of the normalized base choice. Let $RNBI_c$ be the relative nation brand index of country c to the United States (the reference country)—the ratio of the nation c brand index rating to that of the United States. That is,

$$RNBI_c = \frac{NBI_c}{NBI_{US}} \qquad (1)$$

where NBI_c is a vector of the NBI of country c, and NBI_{US} is a vector of the NBI of the United States.

Moderating Effects

There is ample evidence that sociodemographic variables may moderate the effect of decision making. The model allows sociodemographics to exhibit a differential impact on country of origin and various aspects of nation equity perception. In the model, we focus on the sociodemographic moderating effects from the variables gender and age. This is to segregate the polities at large on the response of the country of origin and nation equity perceptions based on gender and age, aiming for efficiency in targeting the nation-branding strategy.

Furthermore, the model also allows for different methods of decision making, accounting for structural heterogeneity to reflect utility maximization and hierarchical choice processes. In particular, a finite mixture of a mixed logit and nested logit model is estimated. The mixed logit and nested logit are set up first, followed by the proposed mixture model.

Mixed Logit Model

Consider that consumer $j \in (1, 2, \ldots, J)$ chooses a favorite alternative $m \in (1, 2, \ldots, M)$ for purchase occasion k, $k \in (1, 2, \ldots, K)$. The utility of alternative m in purchase occasion k for consumer j is defined as

$$U_{jkm} = \alpha_{jc} + \alpha_{coo} = \alpha_g + \beta X_{km} = \varepsilon_{jkm}. \qquad (2)$$

The utility deterministically comprises the product attribute driven preference, $(\beta X_{km}, \alpha_g)$, the product-related country effect, α_{coo}, and the idiosyncratically non–product-related component, α_{jc}. α_g is the key product attribute preference, whereas X_{km} is a vector of other observed product attributes of alternative m in purchase occasion k, which, for example, may be price and third-party reviews. β is a vector of unknown parameters to be estimated. α_{coo} denotes consumer preference toward country of origin c of the chosen alternative m in time k. This term particularly captures the country-of-origin effect. ε_{jkm} is a random error term that is assumed to follow a Type I extreme value distribution, yielding the familiar multinomial logit model. For the idiosyncratic component, α_{jc} is consumer j's non–product-related preference, which is adjustable according to his perception of nation equity aspects of country c, moderated by his sociodemographic profile, and is defined as

$$\alpha_{jc} = \gamma RNBI_{jc} + \delta Z_j RNBI_{jc}. \qquad (3)$$

$RNBI_{jc}$ is a vector of consumer j's perception of country c competency relative to those of the United States. This will be the normalized value of self-reported nation c brand indexes with respect to the United States. γ is the parameter capturing the main effects of nation equity. Z_j is a vector of consumer j's observed demographic variables including gender and age. δ is the focal vector of unknown parameters to be estimated. This term represents the moderating roles of sociodemographics on nation equity, entailing bendable consumer preference with respect to nation images. In effect, Equation 1 becomes

$$U_{jkm} = \gamma RNBI_{jc} + \delta Z_j RNBI_{jc} + \alpha_{coo} + \alpha_g + \beta X_{km} + \varepsilon_{jkm}. \qquad (4)$$

With the logit framework (McFadden, 1974), the probability of choosing alternative m in purchase occasion k for a consumer j is given by the following:

$$P_{jk}^{logit}(m|\alpha_{jc},\alpha_{coo},\alpha_g,\beta) = \frac{\exp(\alpha_{jc} + \alpha_{coo} + \alpha_g + \beta X_{km})}{\sum_{n=1}^{4} \exp(\alpha_{jc} + \alpha_{coo} + \alpha_g + \beta X_{kn})}. \qquad (5)$$

Unobserved Heterogeneity in Country-of-Origin and Key Product Attribute Preferences

To account for heterogeneity across consumers, a random effect model is applied. The country-of-origin preference α_{jcoo} is assumed to be normally distributed with mean $\bar{\alpha}_{jcoo}$ and variance $\sigma^2_{\alpha_{coo}}$, respectively, as follows:

$$\alpha_{jcoo} \sim N(\bar{\alpha}_{coo}, \sigma^2_{\alpha_{coo}}). \qquad (6)$$

Similarly, The key product attribute preference α_{jg} is assumed to be normally distributed with mean $\bar{\alpha}_{jg}$ and variance $\sigma^2_{\alpha_g}$, respectively, as follows:

$$\alpha_{jg} \sim N(\bar{\alpha}_{cg}, \sigma^2_{\alpha_{cg}}). \tag{7}$$

The unconditional choice probability may be written as:

$$P_{jk}^{mlogit}(m) = \iint P_{jk}^{logit}(m|\gamma, \delta, \alpha_{jcoo}, \alpha_{jg}, \beta) f(\alpha_{jcoo}, \alpha_{jg}) d\alpha_{jcoo} d\alpha_{jg} \tag{8}$$

where $f(\alpha_{jcoo}, \alpha_{jg})$ is the joint probability density function of the normal distributions of α_{jcoo} and α_{jg}. By allowing for unobserved heterogeneity, the logit becomes mixed logit (McFadden and Train, 2000).

Nested Logit Model Framework

Because consumers are likely to substitute an alternative with another of the same attribute, let us consider consumers' hierarchical decision process according to the nested logit framework (Forinash and Koppelman, 1993; Lee, 1999) as follows.

Conditional on each purchase occasion k, a consumer chooses alternatives that meet his favorite attribute criterion g. Next, the consumer makes a choice from the subset of alternatives based on other variables. The unconditional probability that a consumer chooses alternative m in purchase occasion k, $P_{jk}(m)$, may be expressed as the product of the probability that the consumer is looking for the key product attribute g, $P_{jk}(g)$, and the probability that the consumer chooses alternative m from a subset of alternatives with the key product attribute g, $P_{jk}(m|g)$:

$$P_{jk}^{nlogit}(m) = P_{jk}(m|g) P_{jk}(g) \tag{9}$$

where

$$P_{jk}(g) = \frac{exp(\alpha_g + \lambda_g I_{jkg})}{\sum_{l=1}^{L} exp(\alpha_l + \lambda_l I_{jkl})}. \tag{10}$$

$$P_{jk}(m|g) = \frac{exp[(\alpha_{coo} + \gamma RNBI_c + \delta Z_j RNBI_c + \beta X_{km})/\lambda_g]}{\sum_{n \in g} exp[(\alpha_{coo} + \gamma RNBI_c + \delta Z_j RNBI_c + \beta X_{kn})/\lambda_g]}. \quad (11)$$

X_{km} is a vector of other observed attributes of alternative m in purchase occasion k. β is a vector of unknown parameters to be estimated. λ_g is an unknown parameter to be estimated that measures correlation among unobserved factors for alternatives with the same attribute g value. α_g is consumer preference for the screening attribute g. α_{coo} denotes consumers' preference for choices from country c that is chosen on purchase occasion k. This term particularly captures the country-of-origin effect. $RNBI_{jc}$ is a vector of consumer j's perception of country c competency relative to those of the United States. This will be the normalized value of self-reported nation c brand indexes with respect to the United States. γ is the parameter capturing the main effects of nation equity. Z_j is a vector of consumer j's observed demographic variables including gender and age. δ is the focal vector of unknown parameters to be estimated. This term represents the moderating roles of sociodemographics on nation equity, entailing bendable consumer preference with respect to nation images. Finally, I_{jkg} represents the inclusive value, which is expressed as follows:

$$I_{jkg} = ln \sum_{n \in g} exp[(\alpha_{coo} + \gamma RNBI_c + \delta Z_j RNBI_c + \beta X_{kn})/\lambda_g]. \quad (12)$$

Note that, like the mixed logit model, the utility deterministically comprises product attribute-driven preference, (βX_{km}, α_g), the product-related country effect, α_{coo}, and the idiosyncratically nonproduct-related component, ($\gamma RNBI_{jc}$, $\delta Z_j RNBI_{jc}$).

Finite Mixture of Nested Logit and Mixed Logit Models

To allow for structural heterogeneity in decision, a finite mixture of the mixed logit and the nested logit models is estimated using an approach similar to that of Kamakura and Russell (1989). The mixed logit represents heterogeneous consumers who evaluate all alternatives at once based on overall satisfaction. In contrast, the nested logit model considers those who adopt a hierarchical decision choice process. This refers to consumers who exhibit substitution among choices of the same criterion. Choices are eliminated based on screening criterion before making the final decision. The log-likelihood function of the mixture model thereby is given as follows:

$$lnL = \sum_j ln(\prod_k \prod_m [P_{jk}^{mlogit}(m)]^{y_{jkm}} \pi_{mlogit} + \prod_k \prod_m [P_{jk}^{nlogit}(m)]^{y_{jkm}} \pi_{nlogit}) \qquad (13)$$

where y_{jkm} is an indicator that has a value of 1 when consumer j chooses alternative m on purchase occasion k; otherwise, 0. ϖ_{nlogit} and ϖ_{mlogit} are parameters to be estimated that represent the proportion of consumers who make decisions according to the nested logit and the mixed logit frameworks, respectively. Parameter estimation was using the R programming language.

Empirical Results

The calibration sample was used to estimate the proposed model in Equations 8–13. Table 11.4 shows parameter estimates of the model. In addressing the perceived nation competence effects on consumer preference, the model attempted to capture various aspects of nation equity. However, we find *relative exports* and *culture* ratings to be the best candidates in estimating the model. In general, a strong preference for the United States as country of origin over that of South Korea prevails. This finding indicates that American TV series benefit from their dominant country-of-origin characteristic, whereas South Korean TV series suffer from a negative country-of-origin effect. Aspects of nation equity work differently among countries. Essentially, *relative Thai exports* is the significant nation equity aspect that respondents embrace for evaluating Thai cultural product whereas *relative South Korean culture* is important for South Korean cultural

Table 11.4

Finite Mixture Model Parameter Estimates, Standard Errors, and *t*-Statistic

	Finite Mixture Model						
	Mixed Logit Segment			Nested Logit Segment			
Parameters	Estimate	Std Err	Est/Std Err	Estimate	Std Err	Est/Std Err	
Genre							
Romantic comedy	**0.857**	0.092	9.370	**0.119**	0.045	2.616	
Period	**−0.294**	0.089	−3.315	**−0.143**	0.046	−3.077	
Action†	**−0.563**	0.097‡	−5.778	0.024	0.092‡	0.260	
County of Origin							
South Korea	**−1.968**	0.671	−2.932	**−0.590**	0.154	−3.829‡	
Std (South Korea)	0.121	0.136	0.885				
Thailand	−0.533	0.342	−1.559	**−0.274**	0.118	−2.328	
Std (Thailand)	0.107	0.162	0.663				
United States†	**2.501**	0.685‡	3.649	**0.864**	0.165‡	5.222	
Relative National Brand Index							
Relative South Korean Exports	0.352	0.852	0.413	0.017	0.149	0.117	
Relative South Korean Culture	**1.404**	0.501	2.802	**0.349**	0.110	3.162	
Relative Thai Exports	**2.835**	0.660	4.293	**0.223**	0.102	2.181	
Relative Thai Culture	**−1.463**	0.575	−2.546	0.145	0.088	1.635	
Moderating Effects of Demographics							
Female*Relative South Korean Exports	**1.832**	0.409	4.483	−0.198	0.108	−1.841	
Male*Relative South Korean Exports†	**−1.832**	0.409	−4.483	0.198	0.108‡	1.841	
< 18*Relative South Korean Exports	−1.948	1.408	−1.384	0.104	0.173	0.605	
18–25*Relative South Korean Exports	**2.293**	0.653	3.512	−0.376	0.218	−1.725	
26–35*Relative South Korean Exports	−0.120	0.863	−0.139	**0.374**	0.183	2.038	

>35*Relative South Korean Exports†	−0.225	0.711‡	−0.303	−0.102	0.213‡	−0.478
Female*Relative South Korean Culture	**−1.014**	0.303	−3.344	0.154	0.093	1.654
Male*Relative South Korean Culture†	**1.014**	0.303‡	3.344	*−0.154*	0.093‡	−1.654
<18*Relative South Korean Culture	1.872	1.244	1.505	−0.100	0.159	−0.627
18–25*Relative South Korean Culture	**−1.730**	0.529	−3.271	0.214	0.163	1.311
26–35*Relative South Korean Culture	−0.230	0.722	−0.319	−0.162	0.159	−1.020
>35*Relative South Korean Culture†	0.088	1.420‡	0.062	0.048	0.178‡	0.267
Female*Relative Thai Exports	*−0.667*	0.356	−1.870	**0.156**	0.078	1.995
Male*Relative Thai Exports†	*0.667*	0.356‡	1.870	**−0.156**	0.078‡	−1.995
<18*Relative Thai Exports	**3.633**	1.611	2.255	0.041	0.127	0.325
18–25*Relative Thai Exports	**−3.992**	0.745	−5.358	0.208	0.140	1.482
26–35*Relative Thai Exports	**3.091**	0.891	3.470	**−0.293**	0.145	−2.011
>35*Relative Thai Exports†	*−2.732*	1.406‡	1.943	0.043	0.184‡	0.234
Female*Relative Thai Culture	0.217	0.238	0.909	−0.100	0.064	−1.557
Male*Relative Thai Culture†	−0.217	0.238‡	−0.909	0.100	0.064‡	1.557
<18*Relative Thai Culture	**−3.248**	1.533	−2.119	0.071	0.105	0.674
18–25*Relative Thai Culture	**2.739**	0.601	4.558	−0.074	0.109	−0.682
26–35*Relative Thai Culture	**−1.339**	0.678	−1.974	−0.005	0.122	−0.045
>35*Relative Thai Culture†	1.847	1.184‡	1.560	0.009	0.142‡	0.064
Reviews						
Positive review	**0.846**	0.070	12.016	**0.209**	0.025	8.381
Negative review†	**−0.846**	0.070‡	−12.016	**−0.209**	0.025‡	−8.381
Favorite Stars						
Favorite stars	**0.575**	0.061	9.390	**0.120**	0.022	5.519
No favorite stars†	**−0.575**	0.061‡	−9.390	**−0.120**	0.022‡	−5.519
1 − λ						
Romantic comedy				**0.421**	0.092	4.563
Period				**0.382**	0.098	3.881
Action				0.052	0.118	0.437

Note: Significant coefficients at alpha = 0.50 and 0.1 are in boldface and italic, respectively; †Effects coding variables; ‡Calculated by the delta method.

products. Overall, results show that nation equity enhances cultural good preference especially when country-of-origin is not preferred. In particular, *relative culture* equity of South Korea to the United States is found to alleviate the negative South Korean country-of-origin effect (–0.59,–1.968). Likewise, *relative export* and *culture* of Thailand to the United States strengthens the volatile positioning of Thai country-of-origin (–0.274). Interestingly, the effects of nation equity vary across age groups and gender. Consistent with the previous findings, the country of origin exhibits a significant effect on preference. This finding shows that both country of origin and nation equity affect decision processes.

The results show that variations exist in decision-making processes. Hierarchical decision choice processes have been well recognized by the nested model with a size of 72 percent, whereas the utility-maximizing counterpart has a 28 percent share size of the mixed logit model. *For the utility-maximizing decision maker,* the country of origin factor is significant and varies across consumers. Respondents prefer TV series from *the United States* (2.501) *and South Korea* (–1.968). The country-of-origin effect of *Thailand* is not significant. Respondents in this segment are very similar in terms of preference in country-of-origin. The South Korean *culture* perception has an impact across age and gender. In particular, this effect is positive with males (1.014) and negative with females (–1.014) and 18–25-year-olds (–1.730). The relative South Korean *export* perception, however, enhances the popularity of South Korean TV series among females (1.832) and the 18–25 age group (2.293), but the reverse is true for males (–1.832).

The findings confirm that *relative Thai exports* is the nation competence that helps to shape Thai TV series preference. Nevertheless, the effect is moderated favorably among males (0.667), those younger than 18 (3.633), and 26–35-year-olds (3.091) but adversely among females (–0.667), the 18–25 age group (–3.992) and the over-35 group (–2.732). Thai TV series' attractiveness may be significantly enhanced via *relative Thai culture*. The perception of relative Thai culture more strongly encourages the selection of

Thai TV series among the 18–25 age group (2.739), but less for the under-18 age group (–3.248) and 26–35 age group (–1.339). Respondents in this decision group are found to prefer *romantic comedy* (0.857), *period* (–0.294), and *action* (–0.563) respectively. *Positive review* and *favorite stars* are significant and encourage choice selection as expected.

For the hierarchical decision choice processor, the results suggest that respondents initially create a subset of choices or nest based on genre before considering other factors. *Romantic comedy* (0.119) is preferred to *period* (–0.143) as genre-selecting criteria. Specifically, the statistic $1-\lambda_g$, which measures the correlation of preferences for alternatives with the same genre, is found to be statistically significant for *romantic comedy* (0.421) and *period* (0.382). In terms of country-of-origin, *the United States* (0.864) is ahead of *South Korea* (–0.59). *Relative South Korean culture* helps to significantly boost the preference for South Korean TV series. This effect is reinforced among female consumers (0.154) but somewhat attenuated among male respondents (–0.154). In addition, *relative South Korean exports* fosters the preference for South Korean TV series among the 26–35 age group (0.374) and male consumers (0.198) while decreasing their attractiveness to females (–0.198) and those age 18–25 (–0.376). Thai TV series are affected not only by *relative Thai exports* (0.223) but also by *relative Thai culture* (0.145). Due to the moderating effects of relative Thai exports, females are found to be more fond of Thai TV series (0.156), whereas the effect is the reverse among males (–0.156) and the 26–35 age group (–0.293). *Positive review* and *favorite star* generally foster the preference for a TV series, as expected.

Model Comparison and Predictive Validity

To validate and test the predictive fit of the proposed model, alternative models such as the mixed logit and the nested logit are estimated (see Table 11.5). Furthermore, we applied the estimated models to the holdout sample of 169 respondents for a total of 1,521 profile sets. Table 11.6 reports predictive validity across models. In particular, the predictive validity assessment is based

Table 11.5

Nested Logit and Mixed Logit Models Parameter Estimates, Standard Errors, and *t*-Statistic

	Mixed Logit Segment			Finite Mixture Model Nested Logit Segment			Nested Logit Segment		
Parameters	Estimate	Std Err	Est/Std Err	Estimate	Std Err	Est/Std Err			
Genre									
Romantic comedy	0.249	0.033	7.595	0.240	0.037	6.443			
Std(Romantic comedy)				0.439	0.044	9.924			
Period	−0.170	0.036	−4.783	−0.185	0.034	−5.373			
Std(Period)				0.243	0.057	4.255			
Action†	−0.079	0.040‡	−1.947	−0.055	0.041‡	−1.335			
County of Origin									
South Korea	−0.752	0.125	−6.038	−0.828	0.161	−5.155			
Std (South Korea)				0.284	0.052	5.474			
Thailand	−0.375	0.102	−3.673	−0.417	0.132	−3.174			
Std (Thailand)				0.289	0.050	5.738			
United States†	1.127	0.141‡	8.012	1.245	0.183‡	6.806			
Relative National Brand Index									
Relative South Korean Exports	0.226	0.117	1.927	0.258	0.153	1.690			
Relative South Korean Culture	0.381	0.090	4.226	0.402	0.116	3.453			
Relative Thai Exports	0.234	0.092	2.547	0.274	0.125	2.186			
Relative Thai Culture	0.218	0.075	2.900	0.240	0.102	2.349			
Moderating Effects of Demographics									
Female*Relative South Korean Exports	0.008	0.084	0.100	−0.049	0.110	−0.442			
Male*Relative South Korean Exports†	−0.008	0.084‡	−0.100	0.049	0.110‡	0.442			
<18*Relative South Korean Exports	−0.278	0.150	−1.855	−0.296	0.191	−1.554			
18–25*Relative South Korean Exports	0.168	0.129	1.305	0.218	0.169	1.290			
26–35*Relative South Korean Exports	0.148	0.154	0.962	0.180	0.200	0.900			
>35*Relative South Korean Exports†	−0.038	0.168‡	−0.228	−0.102	0.223‡	−0.458			

Variable	β	SE	t	β	SE	t
Female*Relative South Korean Culture	0.068	0.073	0.930	0.123	0.097	1.269
Male*Relative South Korean Culture†	−0.068	0.073‡	−0.930	−0.123	0.097‡	−1.269
<18*Relative South Korean Culture	0.220	0.137	1.606	0.262	0.174	1.504
18–25*Relative South Korean Culture	−0.172	0.109	−1.582	−0.250	0.144	−1.736
26–35*Relative South Korean Culture	−0.077	0.132	−0.582	−0.094	0.172	−0.548
>35*Relative South Korean Culture†	0.029	0.139‡	0.212	0.081	0.184‡	0.441
Female*Relative Thai Exports	0.125	0.070	1.783	0.149	0.095	1.576
Male*Relative Thai Exports†	−0.125	0.070‡	−1.783	−0.149	0.095‡	−1.576
<18*Relative Thai Exports	**0.277**	0.123	2.258	0.290	0.163	1.782
18–25*Relative Thai Exports	**−0.262**	0.107	−2.444	**−0.314**	0.147	−2.126
26–35*Relative Thai Exports	0.071	0.129	0.553	0.148	0.176	0.841
>35*Relative Thai Exports†	−0.087	0.159‡	−0.548	−0.124	0.222‡	−0.561
Female*Relative Thai Culture	**−0.123**	0.056	−2.219	−0.132	0.075	−1.753
Male*Relative Thai Culture†	**0.123**	0.056‡	2.219	0.132	0.075‡	1.753
<18*Relative Thai Culture	−0.092	0.102	−0.903	−0.099	0.137	−0.725
18–25*Relative Thai Culture	**0.219**	0.081	2.704	**0.226**	0.112	2.375
26–35*Relative Thai Culture	−0.151	0.102	−1.481	−0.226	0.140	−1.616
>35*Relative Thai Culture†	0.024	0.124‡	0.190	0.059	0.172‡	0.342
Reviews						
Positive review	**0.310**	0.021	14.731	**0.369**	0.020	17.991
Negative review†	**−0.310**	0.021‡	−14.731	**−0.369**	0.020‡	−17.991
Favorite Stars						
Favorite stars	**0.202**	0.018	11.148	**0.234**	0.020	11.816
No favorite stars†	**−0.202**	0.018‡	−11.148	**−0.234**	0.020‡	−11.816
1 − λ						
Romantic comedy	**0.281**	0.074	3.797			
Period	**0.263**	0.080	3.287			
Action	0.020	0.091	0.217			

Note: Significant coefficients at alpha = 0.50 and 0.1 are in boldface and italic, respectively; †Effects coding variables; ‡Calculated by the delta method.

Table 11.6

Predictive Validity

Model	In-sample fit		Out-of-sample fit
	Log likelihood	CAIC	Hit rate
Nested logit	−3,783	7,696	44.8%
Mixed logit	−3,736	7,602	44.2%
Finite mixture	−3,653	7,570	43.3$

on Consistent Akaike Information Criterion (CAIC) and the fitted log-likelihood in sample fit. The hit rate (% of correct choice predictions) is used to evaluate the predictive validity assessment of out-of-sample fit. The proposed model outperforms alternative models for in-sample fit. Under the hit-rate criterion, three models are predictively similar.

Discussion and Conclusion

In this study, we have proposed and investigated empirically how nation equity helps form the consumer preference structure in addition to the country of origin. Specifically, the mixture of the nested logit and mixed logit model is a useful tool for estimating the preference structure across age and genders.

The empirical results for conjoint choice data on TV series demonstrate that the model recognizes two different patterns of decision processes—hierarchical decision-making and utility maximization. In addition to country-of-origin, *Culture and Heritage* and *Exports* are the key nation competence aspects in influencing cultural product preferences. The effects are detected as relative, not absolute, values. In particular, it is a nation's competence relative to that of the reference country. Moderating effects of the two aspects on age and gender are found. Overall, the perceived nation equity makes preferences become malleable and varies across polities. We find this result because perceptions of nation equity may be influenced by nation-branding campaigns and thus are not fixed. If any country changes the nation equity perception of consumers, the country may influence their preference regarding its product. Given the evidence that different consumer profiles and segments respond to nation equity differently, mass nation-branding campaigns should be designed with care.

The question is how to turn nation equity into economic productivity. The difficulty is that a positive nation competence perception does not guarantee that the consumer will choose your product. For example, the NBI survey suggests that Thais have a positive perception of their *culture*. The results, however, show that *relative Thai culture* has positive and negative effects on choice, meaning that there are groups of Thai consumers who not only appreciate but also devalue the Thai cultural aspect of Thai products. Meanwhile, South Korea is very successful in exporting its culture. Notice that there are positive main effects of *relative South Korean culture* in both decision segments. Thai consumers have thus embraced South Korean culture, enhancing South Korean cultural product adoption. This finding helps to reinforce the K-Wave's economic success.

In sum, this study finds that consumers will like their product more if their perceived relative nation competence is growing. In this way, nation equity can translate into monetary value. Therefore, countries suffering from a negative country-of-origin effect can recover their nation images by maneuvering nation equity positioning. Influencing consumer preference via nation equity is thus an effective tool for managing the cultural economy. Note that this study is based on Thai data. It would be interesting to investigate consumer behavior from other countries and categories in future research.

References

Agrawal, J., and Kamakura, W.A. (1999). Country of origin: A competitive advantage? *International Journal of Research in Marketing,* 16, 255–267.
Anholt, S. (2005). Anholt nation brands index: How does the world see America? *Journal of Advertising Research,* 45(3), 296–304.
———. (2007). *Competitive identity: The new brand management for nations, cities, and regions.* Trowbridge, Wilts, UK: Cromwell Press.
Appadurai, A. (1996). *Modernity at large: Cultural dimensions of globalization.* Minneapolis: University of Minnesota Press.
Aronczyk, M. (2009). How to do things with brands: Uses of national identity. *Canadian Journal of Communication,* 34, 291–296.
Batra, R., Ramaswamy, V., Alden, D.L., Steenkamp, J.-B.E.M., and Ramachander, S. (2000). Effects of brand local and nonlocal origin on consumer attitudes in developing countries. *Journal of Consumer Psychology,* 9(2), 83–95.

Ben-Zion, U., and Donnenfeld, S. (1983). Exports as a signal of quality: A new approach to dumping. *Economics Letters*, 13, 373–378.
Bilkey, W.J., and Nes, E. (1982). Country-of-origin effects on product evaluations. *Journal of International Business Studies*, 13(1), 89–99.
Chao, P. (1993). Partitioning country of origin effects: Consumer evaluations of a hybrid product. *Journal of International Business Studies*, 24(2), 291–306.
Diamantopoulos, A., Schelegelmich, B., and Palihawadana, D. (2011). The relationship between country-of-origin image and brand image as drives of purchase intentions: A test of alternative perspectives. *International Marketing Review*, 28(5), 508–524.
Dinnie, K. (2008). *Nation branding: Concepts, issues, practice.* Amsterdam: Elsevier.
Elliot, G.R., and Cameron, R.C. (1994). Consumer perception of product quality and the country-of-origin effect. *Journal of International Marketing*, 2(2), 49–62.
Ettenson, R. (1993). Brand name and country of origin effects in the emerging market economies of Russia, Poland and Hungary. *International Marketing Review*, 10(5), 14–36.
Forinash, C., and Koppelman, F. (1993). Application and interpretation of nested logit models of intercity mode choice. *Transportation Research Record*, 1413, 98–106.
Forster, A. (2012). "Korean wave" brings Asian pop culture to American shores. *Asia Matters for America*, February 2. www.asiamattersforamerica.org/korea/korean-wave-brings-asian-pop-culture-to-american-shores/ (accessed July 15, 2012).
Globalization101.org. (2012). Culture and globalization. www.globalization101.org/category/issues-in-depth/culture/ (accessed July 31, 2012).
Gurhan-Canli, Z., and Maheswaran, D. (2000). Cultural variations in country of origin effects. *Journal of Marketing Research*, 37(3), 309–317.
Han, M., and Terpstra, V. (1988). Country-of-origin effects for uni-national and bi-national products. *Journal of International Business Studies*, 19(2), 235–255.
Hong, S.-T., and Kang, D.K. (2006). Country-of-origin influences on product evaluations: The impact of animosity and perceptions of industriousness on judgments of typical and atypical products. *Journal of Consumer Psychology*, 16(3), 232–239.
Hong, S.-T., and Wyer, R.S., Jr. (1989). Effects of country-of-origin and product-attribute information on product evaluation: An information processing perspective. *Journal of Consumer Research*, 16(2), 175–187.
Jin, D.Y. (2012). Hallyu 2.0: The new Korean wave in the creative industry. *University of Michigan International Journal*, Fall, 3–7.
Kamakura, W.A., and Russell, G. (1989). A probabilistic choice model for market segmentation and elasticity structure. *Journal of Marketing Research*, 26, 379–390.
Klein, J.G., Ettenson, R., and Morris, M.D. (1998). The animosity model of foreign product purchase: An empirical test in the People's Republic of China. *Journal of Marketing*, 62(1), 89–100.
Korea Tourism Organization. (2013). Visitor arrivals, Korean departures, inter-

national tourism receipts and expenditures. http://kto.visitkorea.or.kr/eng/tourismStatics/keyFacts/visitorArrivals.kto (accessed May 17, 2014).
Krishna, R.M. (2010). Problem of identity in globalization. http://www.articlesbase.com/philosophy-articles/problem-of-identity-in-globalization-1672812.html (accessed July 31, 2012).
Lee, B. (1999). Calling patterns and usage of residential toll service under self-selecting tariffs. *Journal of Regulatory Economics,* 16, 45–82.
Maheswaran, D. (1994). Country of origin as a stereotype: Effects of consumer expertise and attribute strength on product evaluations. *Journal of Consumer Research,* 21(2), 354–365.
Maheswaran, D., and Chen, C.Y. (2006). Nation equity: Incidental emotions in country-of-origin effects. *Journal of Consumer Research,* 33(3), 370–376.
———. (2009). Nation equity: Country-of-origin effects and globalization. In M. Kotabe and K. Helsen (Eds.), *SAGE Handbook of International Marketing,* 91–113. Sage.
McFadden, D. (1974). Conditional logit analysis of qualitative choice behavior. In P. Zarembka (Ed.), *Frontiers in Econometrics,* 105–142. New York: Academic Press.
McFadden, D., and Train, K. (2000). Mixed MNL models of discrete response. *Journal of Applied Econometrics,* 15, 447–470.
Nattavuthisit, K., Prasarnphanich, P., and Jindahra, P. (2010). *The dynamic of global culture and its effects on Thailand's culture and society.* Study Report, Bangkok: Thailand's Office of the National Economic and Social Development Board.
Pecotich, A., and Rosenthal, M.J. (2001). Country of origin, quality, brand and consumer ethnocentrism. *Journal of Global Marketing,* 15(2), 31–60.
Profeta, A., Balling, R., and Roosen, J. (2012). The relevance of origin information at the point of sale. *Food Quality and Preference,* 26, 1–11.
Schooler, R. (1971). Bias phenomena attendant to the marketing of foreign goods in the U.S. *Journal of International Business Studies,* 2(1), 71–81.
Shy, O. (2000). Exporting as a signal for product quality. *Economica,* 67, 79–90.
Tomlinson, J. (2003). Globalization and cultural identity. In D. Held and A. McGrew (Eds.), *The global transformation reader,* Vol. 2, 269–277. Cambridge, UK: Polity Press.
UNCTAD. (2013). Trade in creative products reached new peak in 2011, UNCTAD figures show. http://unctad.org/en/pages/newsdetails.aspx?OriginalVersionID=498 (accessed July 31, 2012).
UNDP. (2004). Human development report 2004: Cultural liberty in today's diverse world. New York: UNDP.
UNESCO. (2005). *International flows of selected cultural goods and services, 1994–2003.* Montreal: UNESCO Institute for Statistics.
Verlegh, P.W.J., Steenkamp, J.-B.E.M., and Meulenberg, M.T.G. (2005). Country-of-origin effects in consumer processing of advertising claims. *International Journal of Research in Marketing,* 22, 127–139.
World Bank. (2003). Urban development needs creativity: How creative industries affect urban areas. *Development Outreach,* November.

12

Consumer Self-Connections to Global Brands in Asia

SUNMYOUNG CHO

According to Webster's Dictionary, *Connection* generally means "the act of connecting or the state of being connected as causal or logical relation or sequence." In consumer behavior, the self-brand connection literally means that connections between the consumers self and a brand develop psychologically and more specifically signify that consumers establish special ties with brands and incorporate them into their self-concepts (Escalas and Bettman, 2003). In the context of globalized markets, what does the connection between Asian consumers and Western global brands mean with regard to the two disparate cultures of origin? In addition, what are the consequences of the psychological connections between Asian consumer selves and global brands? This chapter discusses the link between consumer self-connections and global brands and their consequences in Asia, focusing on the formation of self–brand connections at an early age, as shown in personal experiences that exemplify self-enhancing episodes related to global brands and their influence on consumer desire for global cultural consumption and life in the context of the East Asian market.

Consumer Self–Brand Connections and Culture-of-Brand-Origin

Self–brand connection is a central psychological construct in consumer behavior that has been conceptualized as an essential antecedent of the strength of the consumer–brand relationship and a crucial driver of positive brand attitudes and market behaviors

(Aaker, Fournier, and Brasel, 2004; Escalas, 2004; Fournier, 1998; Park et al., 2010; Wuyts, Dekimpe, and Gijsbrechts, 2010). Escalas and Bettman (2003) asserted that consumers can make associations with brands and incorporate them into their self-concepts in the process of constructing relationships with them, and, in so doing, they form psychological connections between the brand and the self, known as *self–brand connections*. Strong connections to brands also involve developmental issues and are used for self-definitional purposes, for example, to negotiate identity and life issues, to share autobiographical values, or to accomplish possible selves (Escalas and Bettman, 2005; Kleine and Baker, 2004; Sirgy, 1982). In addition, the development of self–brand connections can occur in children and adolescents, and its developmental influence on their self-identities and lives has appeared in the literature (Chaplin and John, 2005, 2007).

It has been proposed that in the contemporary global marketplace the culture-of-brand-origin (i.e., global or local) replaces the country-of-origin as an important factor in brand perception and consumer market behavior in the cultural approach to branding (Lim and O'Cass, 2001; Zhou, Yang, and Hui, 2010). Although branding carries a social and interactive mechanism influenced by its cultural contexts (Cayla and Arnould, 2008; McCracken, 2005; Schroeder and Salzer-Mörling, 2006), little is known about consumer self–connection to global brands and the influence of the culture-of-brand-origin on consumption behaviors in the Asian market. If so, how will consumer self-connections to global brands, compared to local brands, affect their identities, lives, and consumer behaviors in Asia?

Connection to Global Brands and Adolescent Yearning for Global Culture

This section, which contains results from the author's qualitative research, offers a glimpse of the meaning behind successful long-term consumer–brand relationships and consumers' lived experiences based on insider perspectives gained in part from in-depth interviews conducted with a group of adult female consumers in

Seoul, Korea (Creswell, 1998; Fournier, 1998; Spradley, 1979; Strauss and Corbin, 1998). Fifty-one interviewees ranging in age from 20 to 60 demonstrated high levels of self–brand connection and long-term positive relationships with specific brands for more than 10 years. Their autobiographical narratives revealed meaningful self-enhancing experiences with focal brands at an early age; participants recalled meaningful episodes vividly and described them clearly as critical moments in their early self–brand connections. Moreover, when the focal brands were Western global brands, key participants expressed that they had developed adolescent yearnings for Western global culture and life; actually, a number of them led global lives with truly cosmopolitan outlooks.

Formation of Self–Brand Connections at an Early Age, the Role of Personal Brand Episode, and Its Development

In accordance with preliminary findings from the brand narratives, one can predict that personally meaningful brand experience at an early age related to global brands can increase consumer desire for global culture, last into adulthood, and affect consumers' lives. In turn, the following empirical studies were designed and conducted, specifically to examine not only the role of meaningful episodes at an early age in the formation of self–brand connections but also their impact on the tendency toward the adoration of global culture and consumption behaviors.

Exploration of Consequences Among Young Adults

A survey was conducted to explore the long-term consequences of the role of meaningful self–brand episodes at an early age in the formation of connections to global (as opposed to local) brands as well as to ascertain the development of desire for global culture and consumption in adulthood. Respondents included 217 young-adult consumers, ranging in age from 19 to 35 and living in Seoul, Korea. Main concepts comprised (a) brand episodes at an early age, favorite brands and the culture of their origin, and interaction between these two variables as independent variables, and (b) self–brand connections, brand attitudes (brand loyalty, willingness to pay premium price, and positive word of mouth [WOM]), adoration of global culture, and tendency toward cosmopolitan consumption as dependent variables (Cleveland and Laroche, 2007; Escalas and Bettman, 2003; Lee, 2009; Shimp, and Sharma, 1987; Yoon, Cannon, and Yarak, 1996). *Adoration of global culture* was defined as consumer interest and passion about culture and consumption in global environments. *Tendency toward cosmopolitan consumption* means the degree of consumers' interest and passion about transnational or cosmopolitan consumption required to fulfill their needs and establish their identities. The use of past and present tense verbs in the questionnaire items was useful in assessing respondents' past experiences and their influence on current attitudes. For analysis, data were divided into two groups by culture-of-brand-origin: Western global brands ($n_1 = 129$) vs. Eastern local brands ($n_2 = 88$). Regression analysis revealed that the more respondents had experienced early meaningful personal brand episodes, the higher their level of self–brand connections and positive brand attitudes. In addition, the more strongly respondents had experienced early meaningful episodes with Western global brands, the higher the level of global culture adoration and tendency toward cosmopolitan consumption, compared to respondents connected with local brands.

Experimental Evidence from Adolescents

An experimental study targeted adolescent consumers to examine the effect of early brand experiences on the formation of connections to global (as opposed to local) brands and to determine whether the experiences would actually evoke the desire for global culture and consumption. A 2 (experience of self–brand episode: experience vs. null) × 2 (culture-of-brand-origin: global vs. local) design was used. Brand episodes for adolescents were secured during visits to four classes of middle school students in Seoul, Korea. The questionnaire used with the middle school students was identical to the one used with the young adults above, with one exception: Present and future tenses were used to determine current desire or attitudes and future intentions and behaviors associated with adolescents' adoration of global culture and tendency toward cosmopolitan consumption. A total of 202 students completed the questionnaire and then participated in a quiz; the questions covered academic and nonacademic knowledge as well as trivia. In this game, 64 students with correct answers received a round of applause and random prizes from two global brands (Ralph Lauren® and Benefit®) and two local brands (Bean Pole® and Etude®), including a daily planner, lip balm, or miniature perfume. Showing off their prizes to parents and friends and talking about their winning experiences was recommended. Two weeks later, the 64 prize winners—that is, the 32 students who received local brands and the 32 who received global brands—were tested again; in addition, a control group comprising 60 participants and divided into two groups by culture-of-brand-origin—that is, global ($n = 31$) vs. local ($n = 29$)—was also tested. As expected, results of analysis of variance (ANOVA) revealed that brand episodes motivated the formation of self–brand connections or alteration of connections to the focal brands awarded as prizes; furthermore, positive brand attitudes naturally increased in both global and local brand winners. Results also demonstrated that connections to global brands following meaningful episodes were likely to increase the level of adoration of global culture and the tendency toward cosmopolitan consumption, but the local brands group showed that the mean level declined slightly and the no-experience group showed no change before and after the quiz. The results can be interpreted as follows: The enhancing experience of a brand episode affects the level of consumer self–brand connections and positive brand attitudes regardless of culture-of-brand-origin, but its impact on the adoration of global culture and tendency toward cosmopolitan consumption are related only to *global brands*.

Cultural Influence of Brands on Consumer Life

This research suggests the critical role of meaningful brand episodes at an early age in the formation of strong self–brand connections and provides initial evidence of relationships between consumers' self-connections to global brand and cultural consumption issues by showing that connections to global (as opposed to local) brands increased the level of desire for global culture and tendency toward cosmopolitan consumption. In addition, results show that the impact of the meaningful brand episodes lasted into adulthood, and its development affected participants' lives over time. Most importantly, the focal prediction of the research emanated from autobiographical brand narratives of particular consumers who had long-term positive relationships with a specific brand for more than 10 years. Maintaining a business for a long time may be difficult, *but it is also not easy retaining customers in the long term who experience friendships with their brands or products.* Especially, consumers with long-term strong brand connections from an early age are valuable assets for branding. Many real phenomena happen in and across time and place. The dyadic perspectives of developmental psychology and the cultural approach to branding provide significant insights based on the time–place interaction of consumer lives in a roundabout way.

Asian Consumers' Connections to Global Brands

The global expansion of top brands, which has accelerated the emergence of a homogeneous global culture, has created a new cultural meaning in everyday life (Cayla and Arnould, 2008; Cleveland and Laroche, 2007; Fournier, 1998). Some Asian consumers develop a passion for culture, transnational or cosmopolitan consumption, their own global life values, and self-enhancing identities when strong connections are formed psychologically between their selves and global brands. Beyond the scope of this chapter is the other side of issue, including excessive materialism or vanity about maintaining a Western image, which can lead to shame and short-lived relationships. According to Webster's Dictionary, *connection* also encompasses "the act or situation in which connecting two or more things have the same cause, origin, goal, etc." That being the case, what else is produced when psychological connections are developed between numerous global brands and Asian young consumers, who integrate them into their identities? Much attention has been paid to the development of future generations and transformative outcomes. The author expects that global brands expanding into Asian markets will accomplish successful businesses through accommodating new trends of the next Asian generation and building valuable connections with Asian consumers.

References

Aaker, J.L., Fournier, S., and Brasel, A.S. (2004). When good brands do bad. *Journal of Consumer Research*, 31, 1–16.
Cayla, J., and Arnould, E.J. (2008). A cultural approach to branding in the global marketplace. *Journal of International Marketing*, 16(4), 86–112.
Chaplin, L.N., and John, D.R. (2005). The development of self-brand connections in children and adolescents. *Journal of Consumer Research*, 32, 119–129.
———. (2007). Growing up in a material world: Age differences in materialism in children and adolescents. *Journal of Consumer Research*, 34(4), 480–493.
Cleveland, M., and Laroche, M. (2007). Acculturation to the global consumer culture: Scale development and research paradigm. *Journal of Business Research*, 60 (3), 249–260.
Creswell, J.E. (1998). *Qualitative inquiry and research design: Choosing among five traditions*. Thousand Oaks, CA: Sage.
Escalas, J.E. (2004). Narrative processing: Building consumer connections to brands. *Journal of Consumer Psychology*, 14(1–2), 168–180.
Escalas, J.E., and Bettman, J.R. (2003). You are what they eat: The influence of reference groups on consumers' connections to brands. *Journal of Consumer Psychology*, 13(3), 339–348.
———. (2005). Self-construal, reference groups, and brand meaning. *Journal of Consumer Research*, 32, 378–389.
Fournier, S. (1998). Consumers and their brands: Developing relationship theory in consumer research. *Journal of Consumer Research*, 24(4), 343–373.
Kleine, S.S., and Baker, S.M. (2004). An integrative review of material possession attachment. *Academy of Marketing Science Review*, 8(4), 1–35.
Lee, J. (2009). Study on tendency of cosmopolitan consumption behavior. Master's thesis, Seoul National University, Seoul, South Korea.
Lim, K., and O'Cass, A. (2001). Consumer brand classifications: An assessment of culture-of-origin versus country-of-origin. *Journal of Product and Brand Management*, 10(2), 120–136.
McCracken, G.D. (2005). *Culture and consumption II: Markets, meaning, and brand management*. Bloomington: Indiana University Press.
Park, C.W., MacInnis, D.J., Priester, J., Eisengerich, A.B., and Iacabucci, D. (2010). Brand attachment and brand attitude strength: Conceptual and empirical differentiation of two critical brand equity drivers. *Journal of Marketing*, 74(6), 1–17.
Schroeder, J.E., and Salzer-Mörling, M. (2006). *Brand culture*. London: Routledge.

Shimp, T.A., and Sharma, S. (1987). Consumer ethnocentrism: Construction and validation of the CETSCALE. *Journal of Marketing Research,* 24 (3), 280–289.

Sirgy, J.M. (1982). Self-concept in consumer behavior: A critical review. *Journal of Consumer Research,* 9(3), 287–300.

Spradley, J.P. (1979). *The ethnographic interview.* New York: Holt, Rinehart, and Winston.

Strauss, A.L., and Corbin, J.M. (1998). *Basics of qualitative research: Techniques and procedures for developing grounded theory.* 2d ed. Los Angeles: Sage.

Wuyts, S., Dekimpe, M.G., and Gijsbrechts, E. (2010). *The connected customer: The changing nature of consumer and business markets.* New York: Taylor & Francis.

Yoon, S.J., Cannon, H., and Yarak, A. (1996). Evaluating the CYMYC cosmopolitanism scale on Korean consumers. *Advances in International Marketing,* 7, 211–232.

Zhou, L., Yang, Z., and Hui, M.K. (2010). Non-local or local brands? A multi-level investigation into confidence in brand origin identification and its strategic implications. *Journal of the Academy of Marketing Science,* 38(2), 202–218.

13

Impact of Spouses' Past Influence Patterns on Economic Decision Making

A Couple's Diary Technique Applied in Vietnamese Households

ELFRIEDE PENZ AND ERICH KIRCHLER

Motivation

In emerging markets, consumers such as the Vietnamese middle class in urban areas are becoming more affluent. Today, consumer spending is an important part of Vietnam's economy (Cohen, 2004; Euromonitor International, 2010). These developments transform families' and individuals' consumption habits. After they become wealthier, consumers tend to spend money on expensive products, such as luxury goods, cars, furniture, and high-end technology (Khanh and Hau, 2007).

Little is known about purchase decision making in emerging markets at the level of private households. We study couples' economic decision-making processes in an emerging market, Vietnam, using a diary technique over a period of three months. This is novel, as husband and wife independently reported their perceptions and behaviors during decision-making processes by filling in the structured diary every day. This allows for dyadic analyses and keeping track of the decision and mutual influence history. In addition, the role in decision making of each spouse can be analyzed.

Conceptualization

When it comes to purchase decisions in Asian culture, close relationships matter. The Vietnamese invest in harmonious and stable relationships and prefer products to be used as social symbols. Long-term family interests are more important than individual interests (Le and Jolibert, 2001). In Vietnam and other transitional countries with a Confucian tradition, the family was long considered an autonomous unit (Fowler, Gao, and Carlson, 2010; Nguyen, Kirk, and Johnson, 2009). From a consumer research perspective, this is relevant to studies on economic decision making.

Households are sites of cooperation, where conflicting interests are often subject to negotiation (Burgoyne and Kirchler, 2008). While economic and consumption habits are changing rapidly, middle-class families appear to be preserving their traditional influence patterns in purchase decisions (Penz and Kirchler, 2012).

In close relationships, the influence on decisions is studied by analyzing interaction patterns and settlement of disagreements in everyday matters and determining the influence of partners on conflicts and decision making. However, the decision dynamics—that is, looking at sequences of decision making and decisions that are interconnected—have largely been neglected in past research. We aim to find out in what topic areas conflicts arise, how they are perceived emotionally, how they affect relationship quality, and what tactics couples use to settle conflicts. With regard to the dynamics of decisions, we investigate whether past decisions influence subsequent decisions—that is, whether balance in influence between partners is established.

Methodology

A diary study based on the Vienna Diary Study was developed consisting of two diary question sheets (Kirchler et al., 2001). The first set of questions related to whether couples talked to each other, what issues they talked about, whether there was (dis)agreement, and how they felt. The overall feeling about the partnership and who contributed more to the partnership were included as well.

The second set of questions related to a specific conflict that was reported. For the conflict, couples independently reported descriptive information (where they were, who was with them, how long the conversation took, etc.) as well as perceptional information about who had more knowledge and influence on the topic, how important the topic was, whether a decision was derived, and so on. In addition, couples had to choose from a list of tactics (Kirchler et al., 2001) that they used in the conflict. In addition to self-reports, the perception of the partner's behavior was indicated as well, allowing for studying the subjective perception of the couple. Participants in the study were asked to fill in the diary every day for three months. A few minutes per day was required to complete the diary sheets.

A total of 52 middle-class couples participated. The couples were approached by a local researcher and received a detailed explanation of the procedure. They were paid US$80 per month for participating. The average participating couple lived with one or two children. Their level of education was above the national average. Women were, on average, 44 years old and men were 48 years old. Both partners were working. On average, couples spent about six hours together, with one hour per day talking to each other.

Major Findings

Couples discussed primarily the topics of children, consumption, spending, and work. They agreed on most topics and reported that feelings during the conversation were average to good. Overall, men felt better, more powerful, and much freer than women in the partnership. Men also indicated that their wives invested more in the partnership than they did. With respect to conflict issues, participants reported overall 3.682 conflicts, which took place mainly at home and lasted for about half an hour on average. Often discussed conflicts related to the household (e.g., appliances: 25.8 percent), children (e.g., education: 22.2 percent), food (e.g., groceries: 16.9 percent), personal expenditures (e.g., clothing: 15.9 percent), luxury goods (e.g., travel: 14.7 percent), and family/friends (e.g., gifts: 4.3 percent).

The relevance of past decision dynamics on actual spouses' influence patterns was tested by hierarchical regression analyses. Various "influence bookkeeping" models were analyzed. First, Vietnamese couples decide mainly based on existing knowledge about a conflict topic: the partner with more knowledge is more influential in the decision. Second, when it comes to patterns of influence, results show that past decisions seem to influence the subsequent decision positively. This means that the person who decided in the past decides in the current situation as well, and no balancing of influence across decisions within couples is achieved. This was particularly true for men, who also had more influence even if their benefit from the decision outcome was low. These results indicate—unlike what was found in a European study (Kirchler et al., 2001)—that partners in Vietnam practice influence segmentation—that is, clear role segmentation between husband and wife. Although decision making seems to be a rather unbalanced activity regarding mutual influence over a period of three months, more variability and balance emerged from looking at smaller time periods.

Results need to be interpreted along the Vietnamese cultural context, which is a masculine-dominated culture in which maintaining or losing face is an important concern. Decision making in close relationships is characterized by clear role differentiation, confirming research on sex-role stereotypes in Vietnam (Penz and Kirchler, 2012).

Acknowledgment

The authors are grateful to Ria Ursula Peterlik for organizing the diary study in Vietnam, supervising the participating couples, and data collection.

References

Burgoyne, C., and Kirchler, E. (2008). Financial decisions in households. In A. Lewis (Ed.), *The Cambridge Handbook of Psychology and Economic Behaviour,* 132–154. Cambridge: Cambridge University Press.

Cohen, M. (2004). New taste for the good life. *Far Eastern Economic Review,* October 28, 44–46.

Euromonitor International. (2010). Regional focus: Asia Pacific presents a sound prospect to businesses thanks to rising disposable income. *Euromonitor International,* April 12.

Fowler, A.R., Gao, J., and Carlson, L. (2010). Public policy and the changing Chinese family in contemporary China: The past and present as prologue for the future. *Journal of Macromarketing,* 30(4), 342–353.

Khanh, N.T.T., and Hau, L.N. (2007). Preferred appeals as a reflection of culture: Mobile phones advertising in Vietnam. *Asia Pacific Business Review,* 13(1), 21–39.

Kirchler, E., Rodler, C., Hölzl, E., and Meier, K. (2001). *Conflict and decision-making in close relationships: Love, money and daily routines.* Hove, UK: Psychology Press.

Le, T.M., and Jolibert, A. (2001). L'influence de la culture Vietnamienne sur le comportement de l'acheteur. *Décisions Marketing,* 22(January–April), 43–52.

Nguyen, T.T.M., Kirk, S., and Johnson, R.C. (2009). Measurement of modern and traditional Self-concepts in Asian transitional economies. *Journal of Asia-Pacific Business,* 10(3), 201–220.

Penz, E., and Kirchler, E. (2012). Sex-role specialization in a transforming market: Empirical evidence from Vietnamese middle-class households. *Journal of Macromarketing,* 32(1), 61–73.

14

Sequential Cross-Sectional Studies of Values in Singapore and the United States

Soo Jiuan Tan, Siok Kuan Tambyah, and Lynn R. Kahle

Social values are among the most important constructs in social science. Rokeach (1973) noted that the "antecedents of human values can be traced to culture, society and its institutions, and personality" (p. 3). Thus, values provide an individual-level measure of the culture and conditions of a society. Rokeach further argued, "the consequences of human values will be manifested in virtually all phenomena that social scientists might consider worth investigating and understanding" (p. 3).

In marketing, we know that social values play a central role in consumer decision making from "means-end chain" research (e.g., Reynolds and Olsen, 2001). If you ask consumers why they bought a particular product, their answer usually focuses on an attribute of the product. If you ask them why that particular attribute matters, consumers will respond by referring to a consequence of the attribute. The consequence, in turn, matters because it relates to a core social value. Thus, when consumers are faced with a difficult decision, they often will look to their core values to help them sort among choices. This same process is invoked in many important decision-making situations. For example, a recent PhD deciding which of two jobs offers to accept will often reflect on which core social values each job might satisfy. We know that values predict consumption decisions ranging from packaging preferences (Limon, Kahle, and Orth, 2009) to travel choices (Matsuura, Stinson, and Kahle, 2012) to international charitable contributions (Michon, Chebat, and Kahle, 2012). Most important for this book, we know that values affect marketing communication response and brand choice, including processing advertisements (see Kahle and Xie, 2008).

A great deal of progress in recent years has helped us develop a more sophisticated view of the influence of values on consumers (Batra, Homer, and Kahle, 2001; Homer and Kahle, 1988; Kahle and Valette-Florence, 2012; Orth and Kahle, 2008). We now know that values guide behaviors through attitudes, that they vary from situation to situation, that they help define lifestyles, and that they interact with other norms in exerting an influence. Values can therefore help facilitate segmentation strategy above and beyond demographic and other psychographic information (Kahle, 1986).

Understanding social values also contributes to geographic marketing because the patterns of values usually differ from place to place (Kahle, 1986; Kahle and Xie, 2008), and they change over time as well (Kahle, Poulos, and Sukhdial, 1988). One way to understand the context of marketing is to contrast social values within different times or different places to grasp the dynamic influences of temporal and geographic effects. A value-linked product or campaign that works well at one time and place may not work as effectively in another time or place if social values differ. Monitoring values over time and place can inform how segments are evolving and how marketing strategies must adapt.

The issue of temporal stability is interesting from a theoretical perspective. Rokeach (1973) defined a value as "an enduring belief" (p. 5), thus implying relative stability in values. At the same time, he conducted experimental manipulations of values that resulted in major changes in values over a short period of time, often a matter of minutes (Ball-Rokeach, Rokeach, and Grube, 1984; Rokeach, 1973), thus implying that values have the potential to change quickly, even if the consequences are enduring. Others have found relative stability in values (Hoge and Bender, 1974; Konty and Dunham, 1997; Newcomb et al., 1967; Stockard, Carpenter, and Kahle, 2014).

One way to study changes in values is through sequential cross-sectional studies. They draw representative samples of populations using the same or similar methods at repeated times, allowing scholars to look at several snapshots of a culture or country and to assess the degree of stability or change within a society. These studies have an advantage over longitudinal studies in that they have built-in corrections for the changing composition of a sampling unit and they do not require keeping track of the movements of mobile individuals.

An interesting pair of sequential cross-sectional studies provided an unique opportunity to look at societal change over time among Asian consumers (Tambyah and Tan, 2013) in Singapore, and among North American consumers (Gurel-Atay et al., 2010) in the United States (United States). The purpose of this chapter is to compare and contrast the findings of those two articles regarding the stability of values. Such an investigation could provide a deeper understanding of the Asian consumer by examining the effects of time and place on values and by highlighting distinctive characteristics.

The method for measuring values in these studies is the List of Values (e.g., Kahle, 1983), which has been used a great deal in marketing (see Kahle, 1996; Kahle and Xie, 2008). The reliability and validity of the List of Values has been documented (e.g., Beatty et al., 1985; Kahle, 1996; Kahle, Beatty, and Homer, 1986; Kahle and Valette-Florence, 2012; Kahle and Xie, 2008). Table 14.1 presents the items from the List of Values. Note that fun and enjoyment in life and excitement are usually collapsed together. Although excitement has had an interesting run in marketing (e.g., Pontiac's tag line, "We build excitement"), it is generally selected by a statistically very small subsample of people.

The Two Research Streams:
Methods and Findings

Gurel-Atay et al. (2010) compared changes in social values in the United States over 30 years with data collected in 1976 (Kahle, 1983), 1986 (Kahle et al., 1988), and 2007 on three separate national

Table 14.1

List of Values

Value	Description
Sense of belonging	To be accepted and needed by your family, friends, and community.
Security	To be safe and protected from misfortune and attack.
Self-respect	To be proud of yourself and confident with who you are.
Warm relationships with others	To have close companionships and intimate friendships.
Fun and enjoyment in life	To lead a pleasurable life.
Being well respected	To be admired by others and to receive recognition.
Sense of accomplishment	To succeed at whatever you do.
Self-fulfillment	To find peace of mind and to make the best use of your talents.
Excitement	To experience stimulation and thrills.

Source: Kahle (1996).

cross-sectional samples. Results are summarized in Table 14.2. They found that self-respect and fun-enjoyment-excitement showed the greatest gain in importance, with self-respect as the most important value. Warm relationships with others and self-fulfillment followed as close seconds in order of importance. Security and sense of belonging demonstrated the most decline. Between 1976 and 2007, only Americans older than 60 years reported a significantly different ranking of values from that of people in 2007. Between 1986 and 2007, there was a reverse pattern in importance placed on different values; thus, more important values in 1986 were perceived as less important in 2007. Note that the respondents were asked to select their first and second most important values from the list of nine survey items, and "fun and enjoyment" and "excitement" were collapsed into a single value for analysis.

Surveys on nationally representative samples in Singapore have

Table 14.2

Values in the United States

	1976 n = 2,233	1986 n = 997	2007 n = 1,498
Self-respect	21.1 (1)	23.0 (1)	28.8 (1)
Security	20.6 (2)	16.5 (3)	12.4 (3)
Warm relationships with others	16.2 (3)	19.9 (2)	20.9 (2)
Sense of accomplishment	11.4 (4)	15.9 (4)	10.3 (4)
Self-fulfillment	9.6 (5)	6.5 (6)	8.1 (7)
Being well-respected	8.8 (6)	5.9 (7)	8.3 (6)
Sense of belonging	7.9 (7)	5.1 (8)	3.3 (8)
Fun-enjoyment-excitement	4.5 (8)	7.2 (5)	9.3 (5)
Total	100%	100%	100%

Note: Numbers are percentages for "Most Important" and Ranks (in parentheses) for 1976, 1986, and 2007.

been conducted measuring social values in 1996, 2001, and 2011 (Kau et al. 2004; Tambyah et al. 2010; and Tambyah and Tan, 2013). In the three surveys (1996, 2001, and 2011), the research used a stratified random sampling approach: For Stage 1, a random selection of a household was used. For Stage 2, selection of an individual within the selected household was used. The minimum-age criterion was 15 years old, slightly younger than in the U.S. samples. Face-to-face surveys via the door-to-door method were used, as was the case in the first U.S. survey. In the second U.S. survey, researchers interviewed respondents from a Market Facts Consumer Mail Panel. For the third U.S. survey, data was collected through an online omnibus survey. The data collection for both Singapore and the United States was carried out by reputable market research firms. The total number of respondents for the three Singapore surveys were approximately 1,500 in each case, slightly smaller than the first U.S. study (2,232) but somewhat larger than in the other two U.S. studies (997, 1,498). It is interesting to note that face-to-face survey methodology has lost its appeal in the United States more quickly than in Singapore because trust in strangers approaching a housing unit in Singapore has not deteriorated as rapidly as in the United States.

Table 14.3 presents the results from the three Singapore studies.

Table 14.3

Values in Singapore (Importance Rankings and Relative Ranks for 1996, 2001, and 2011)

List of values	1996 (rank) n = 1,535	2001 (rank) n = 1,500	2011 (rank) n = 1,500
Self-respect	5.40 (1)	4.83 (1)	5.03 (2)
Security	5.28 (2)	4.72 (5)	5.09 (1)
Being well-respected	5.10 (3)	4.77 (3)	4.88 (7)
Warm relationships with others	5.08 (4)	4.83 (1)	4.99 (3)
Sense of accomplishment	4.94 (5)	4.70 (6)	4.90 (6)
Self-fulfillment	4.83 (6)	4.76 (4)	4.93 (5)
Sense of belonging	4.94 (7)	4.60 (8)	4.98 (4)
Fun and enjoyment	4.79 (8)	4.65 (7)	4.85 (8)
Excitement	4.01 (9)	4.49 (9)	4.44 (9)

Note: Means of scale ranging from 1 = Not important at all to 6 = Very important.

In the United States, "warm relationship with others" increased in importance, but "sense of belonging" demonstrated the most decline over the years both in Singapore and the United States. In the United States, "self-respect" and "self-fulfillment" registered sharp increases over the years (1976–2007). In Singapore, however, "warm relationships with others" increased and then declined. "Self-respect" remained important in Singapore but did not grow as much as in the United States. In the United States, "security" demonstrated the most decline, but "fun-enjoyment- and excitement" showed the greatest gain in importance over the years (1976–2007). In contrast, for Singapore, the importance of "security" has soared.

To provide more insights from the perspective of different age groups of consumers, we take a closer look at the top three values for Singaporeans in 2011 and compare these with Americans. Security has risen in importance across all age groups through the years in Singapore. Older people usually regard security as more important. In the United States, security has declined in importance. In 2007, those people age 40–49 years considered security "very important," but people in their sixties believed that it was not very important. For self-respect in Singapore, there is a sharp increase

Table 14.4

Percentage in United States from 2007 Endorsing Top Three Values of Singapore in 2011 Contrasted by Age

	< 30	30–39	40–49	50–59	60+
Security	11.4	10.6	12.0	8.7	7.8
Self-respect	26.3	30.4	28.6	27.3	30.3
Warm relationships with others	14.4	19.1	17.3	5.8	14.2

for those age 55–64 years while for other age groups it registered a dip in importance. In the United States, dramatic increases were noted for people younger than 30 years, 30–39 years, and over age 60. For "warm relationships with others," there is an increase in importance for all age groups, especially those people age 55–64 years. There is a slight dip for people age 65 years and above. In the United States, there is a drop in importance for people younger than 30 years and people older than 50 years (see Table 14.4 and Figures 14.1–14.3).

Figures 14.4, 14.5, and 14.6 summarize the trends for Singapore

Figure 14.1 **Security, Ranked 1 in 2011** (Singapore Data)

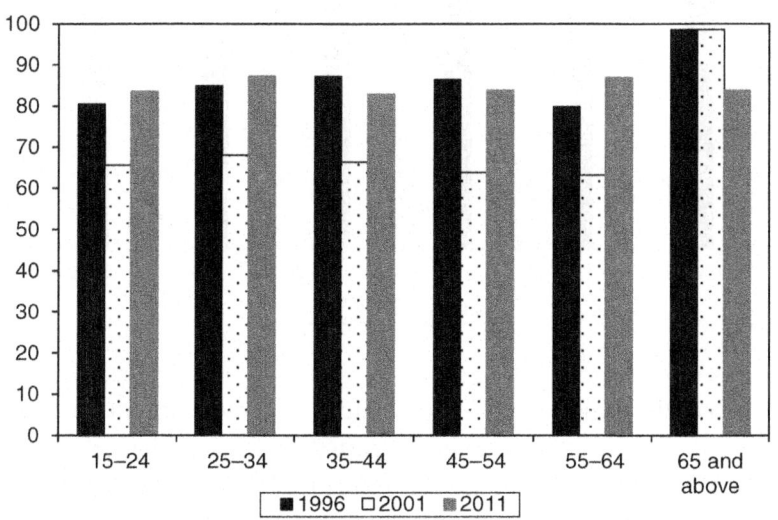

Figure 14.2 **Self-Respect, Ranked 2 in 2011** (Singapore Data)

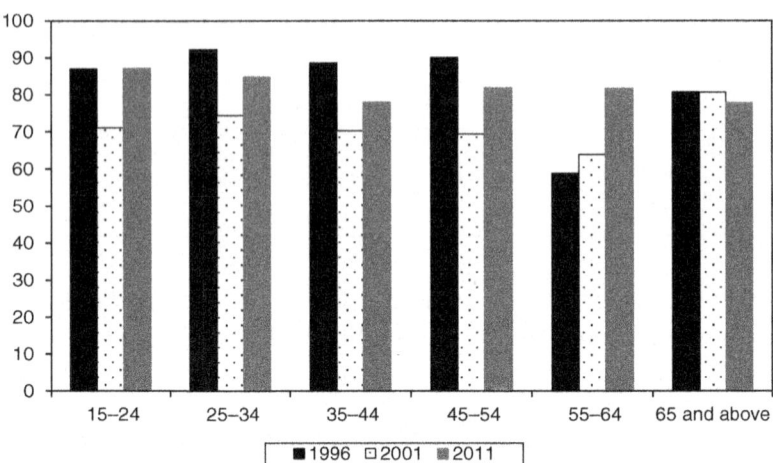

Figure 14.3 **Warm Relationships with Others, Ranked 3 in 2011**
(Singapore Data)

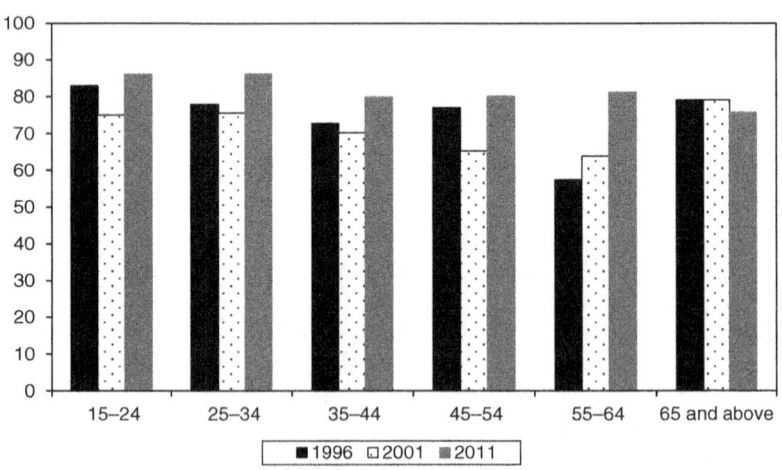

in each of the major categories of values. It is evident that the trends in Singapore within the major categories have been relatively stable. Values with a social dimension (warm relationships with others, being well respected, and sense of belonging) might be expected to

Figure 14.4 **Singapore Values with a Social Dimension** (Singapore Data)

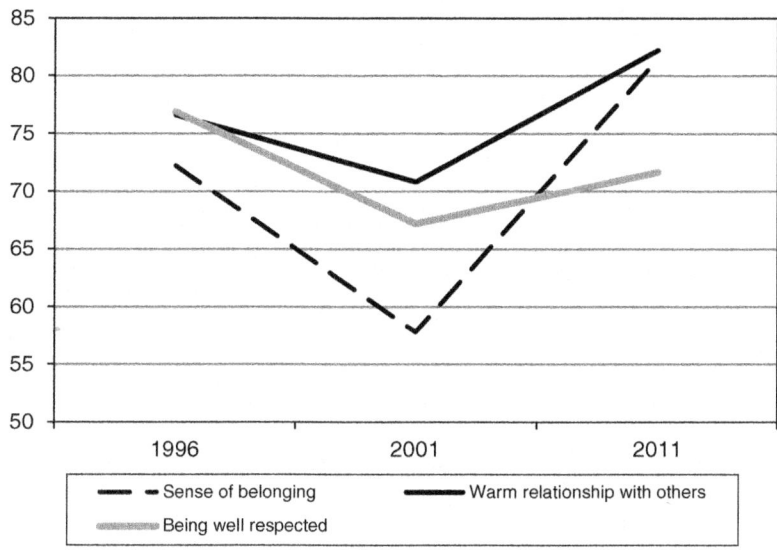

Figure 14.5 **Values with a Pro-/Anti-Hedonism Dimension** (Singapore Data)

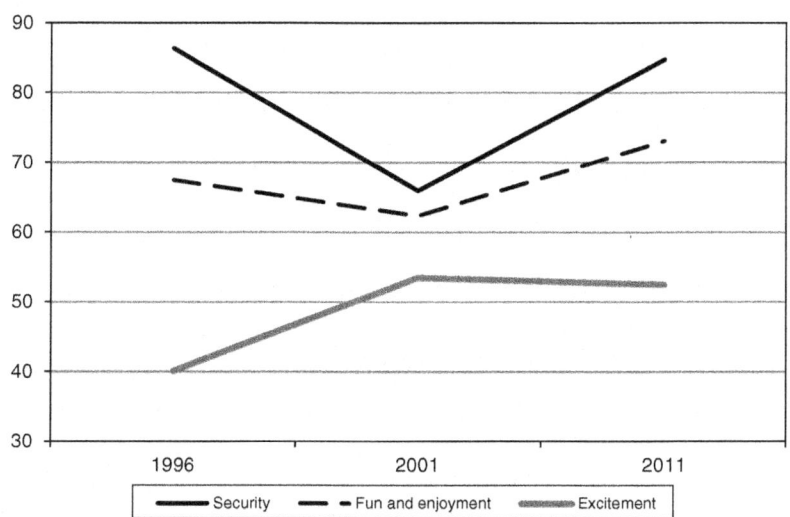

Figure 14.6 **Values with a Self-Oriented Dimension** (Singapore Data)

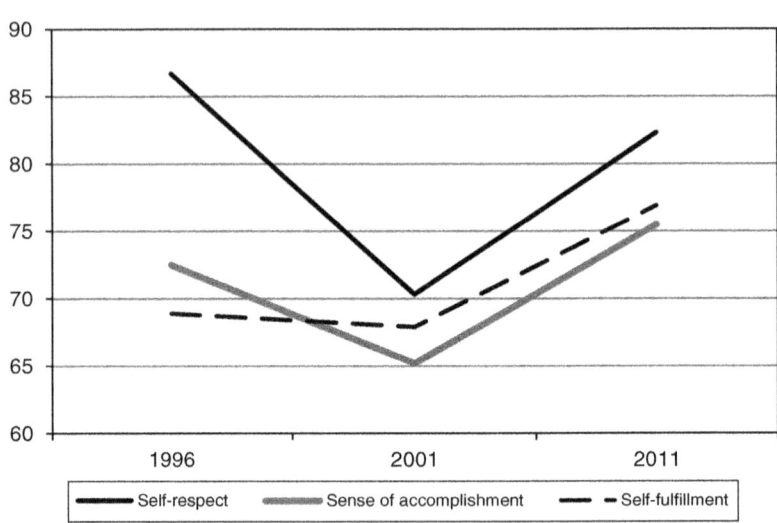

rate more highly in an Asian culture but the ratings of these values may experience downward pressure as secularization transforms the society. Self-respect, sense of accomplishment, and self-fulfillment have a more self-oriented theme, and in an Asian culture one might expect them to be less important but increasing. The more hedonistic values of fun and enjoyment in life, (anti) security, and excitement might be expected to rise as economic prosperity rises, which has happened more dramatically over the past generation in Singapore than in the United States, but pro-security is the new top value in Singapore.

Several major trends warrant comment:

1. Self-respect as the most important value across demographic groups and over the years in both countries might be a consistent and useful theme for formulating marketing communications to resonate with multiple target segments or general audiences. It is prominent in both the United States and in Singapore.
2. Security has become more important in Singapore; hence,

a fear appeal may still be effective in marketing communications there. Generally, extreme fear appeals are not particularly effective, but marketers whose products or services improve security could benefit from this fact in Singapore.
3. Sense of belonging and warm relationship with others as top important values in Singapore suggest that companies should emphasize interpersonal communication, and service firms could incorporate such values in their advertising and promotions.
4. "Being well-respected" has declined significantly in importance in both countries; hence, advertisements using executions that portray consumers trying to get the approval/envy/respect of others may be less effective. Consumers who take control of finding respect and value self-respect, in contrast, are growing in importance.
5. Unlike in the United States, "fun-enjoyment" and "excitement" have remained lowest in importance in Singapore; hence, it may not be effective for marketers to consider incorporating greater entertainment and leisure elements into marketing communications in Singapore, at least as a product or brand benefit.

Conclusion

Marketers need to understand the values of the times and places where they are trying to communicate the benefits of their products and brands. Failure to use current and local information about consumer values could result in unfortunate and unsuccessful efforts at influencing consumers and achieving marketing goals. Marketers must appreciate how values are individual-level representations of cultural perspectives, that different consumers have different views, and that values change constantly with time and place.

A marketer from the United States seeking to enter Singapore, or vice versa, would be wise to study the data presented here in order to understand how their own cultural experiences need to be modified to address the other country's cultural context.

References

Ball-Rokeach, S., Rokeach, M., and Grube, J.W. (1984). *The great American values test: Influencing behavior and belief through television.* New York: Free Press.

Batra, R., Homer, P.M., and Kahle, L.R. (2001). Values, susceptibility to interpersonal influence, and attribute importance weights: A nomological analysis. *Journal of Consumer Psychology,* 11(2), 115–128.

Beatty, S.E., Kahle, L.R., Homer, P., and Misra, S. (1985). Alternative measurement approaches to consumer values: The List of Values and the Rokeach Value Survey. *Psychology and Marketing,* 2(Fall), 181–200.

Gurel-Atay, E., Xie, G.X., Chen, J., and Kahle, L.R. (2010). Changes in social values in the United States, 1976–2007. *Journal of Advertising Research,* 50(1), 57–67.

Hoge, D.R., and Bender, I.E. (1974). Factors influencing value change among college graduates in adult life. *Journal of Personality and Social Psychology,* 29, 572–585.

Homer, P.M., and Kahle, L.R. (1988). A structural equation test of the value-attitude-behavior hierarchy. *Journal of Personality and Social Psychology,* 54(April), 638–646.

Kahle, Lynn R., Ed. (1983). *Social values and social change: Adaptation to life in America.* New York: Praeger.

———. (1986). The nine nations of North America and the value basis of geographic segmentation. *Journal of Marketing,* 50(April), 37–47.

———. (1996). Social values and consumer behavior: Research from the list of values. In C. Seligman, J.M. Olson, and M.P. Zanna (Eds.), *The psychology of values: The Ontario symposium,* Vol. 8, 135–151. Mahwah, NJ: Lawrence Erlbaum.

Kahle, L.R., Beatty, S.E., and Homer, P. (1986). Alternative measurement approaches to consumer values: The list of values (LOV) and values and life style (VALS). *Journal of Consumer Research,* 13(December), 405–409.

Kahle, L.R., Poulos, B., and Sukhdial, A. (1988). Changes in social values in the United States during the past decade. *Journal of Advertising Research,* 28(February–March), 35–41.

Kahle, L.R., and Valette-Florence, P. (2012). *Marketplace lifestyles in an age of social media: Theory and methods.* Armonk, NY: M.E. Sharpe.

Kahle, L.R., and Xie, G.X. (2008). Social values in consumer psychology. In C.P. Haugvedt, P.M. Herr, and F.R. Kardes (Eds.), *Handbook of consumer psychology,* 275–285. Mahwah, NJ: Lawrence Erlbaum.

Kau, A.K, Jung, K., Tambyah, S.K., and Tan, S.J. (2004). *Understanding Singaporeans: Values, lifestyles, aspirations, and consumption behaviors.* Hackensack, NJ: World Scientific.

Konty, M.A., and Dunham, C.C. (1997). Differences in value and attitude change over the life course. *Sociological Spectrum,* 17, 277–197.

Limon, Y., Kahle, L.R., and Orth, U. (2009). Package design as a communications vehicle in cross-cultural values shopping. *Journal of International Marketing,* 17(34), 30–57.

Matsuura, Y., Stinson, J., and Kahle, L.R. (2012). Personality and personal values in travel destination preference. In J.F.B. Lengler and C.A.M. Mello (Eds.), *Personal values and strategic marketing,* 69–81. Santa Cruz do Sul, Brazil: EDUNISC.

Michon, R., Chebat, J.-C., and Kahle, L.R. (2012). Selling brotherhood to North-American multicultural markets: How life values mediate charitable donation behaviors. In J.F.B. Lengler and C.A.M. Mello (Eds.), *Personal values and strategic marketing,* 82–96. Santa Cruz do Sul, Brazil: EDUNISC.

Newcomb, T.M., Koenig, K.E., Flacks, R., and Warwick, D.P. (1967). *Persistence and change.* New York: Wiley.

Orth, U., and Kahle, L.R. (2008). Intrapersonal variation in consumer susceptibility to normative influence: Toward a better understanding of brand choice decisions. *Journal of Social Psychology,* 148(4), 423–447.

Reynolds, T., and Olson, J.C. (2001). *Understanding consumer decision making: The means-end approach to marketing and advertising strategy.* Mahwah, NJ: Lawrence Erlbaum.

Rokeach, M. (1973). *The nature of human values.* New York: Free Press.

Stockard, J., Carpenter, G., and Kahle, L.R. (2014). Continuity and change in values in midlife: Testing the age stability hypothesis. *Experimental Aging Research,* 40(2), 224–244.

Tambyah, S.K, and Tan, S.J. (2013). *Happiness and well-being: The Singaporean experience.* Singapore: Routledge.

Tambyah, S.K, Wirtz, J., and Mattila, A.S. (2010). Organizational learning from customer feedback received by service employees: A social capital perspective. *Journal of Service Management,* 21(3), 363–387.

Tokuda, Y., Fujii, S., and Inoguchi, T. (2010). Individual and country-level effects of social trust on happiness: The Asian barometer survey. *Journal of Applied Social Psychology,* 40, 2574–2593.

Part IV

Current Practices

The chapters in Part IV explore practical applications in a variety of settings, including mobile phone marketing, social media usage, and brand logo design.

Chapter 15, by Mustika Sufiati Purwanegara, Ronny Armando Pitojo, and Mia Tantri Diah Indriani provides a consumer perspective on mobile phone marketing. The authors offers practical advice on how to tackle this increasingly important new medium. As mobile—and smartphone—consumption is a well-established and widespread phenomenon in Asia, a consumer rather than pure technology perspective is critical in understanding the impact of this new technology on consumer attitudes and preferences.

Werner Kunz and Raymond Liu, in Chapter 16, compare Asian and Western users of social media. They focus, in particular, on the type of activities in online platforms and what benefits Chinese and Americans derive from them. They find that the Chinese approach social media more rationally than Americans, for whom social media represent hedonic consumption and entertainment. The chapter has important practical implications for how to design social media in Asia.

The next two chapters examine different facets of brand logo design and consumers' perception of and receptiveness toward different logo design elements. In Chapter 17, Yuwei Jiang, Gerald Gorn, Maria Galli, and Amitava Chattopadhyay show that "shape matters." Examining angular and circular logos, they find that angular logos generally are associated with "hard," whereas circular logos have softer image. They advise companies to pay attention to logo shape and to select logos whose aesthetic properties reinforce the brand image.

Finally, in Chapter 18, Naoko Moriyoshi and Miho Sasaki demonstrate that beyond universal aesthetic elements, individual differences such as consumers' prior exposure to environmental visual stimuli can also influence consumers' liking and acceptance of changes in log design. Considering that companies are constantly looking at revising their brand logos, package designs, and other elements of their corporate visual identify so as to stay relevant in the marketplace, these consumer-centric findings present valuable insights that could guide corporate branding strategy.

As a whole, Part IV illustrates how research in consumer psychology can provide guidance for practical and managerial decisions. That is, when brand managers in Asia face decisions on the fast-expanding mobile marketing and m-commerce space, or media agencies address social media issues, or corporate identity firms need to design logos, they can turn to consumer research to get practical guidance.

15

Consumers' Perspective on Mobile Phone Marketing

MUSTIKA SUFIATI PURWANEGARA,
RONNY ARMANDO PITOJO,
AND MIA TANTRI DIAH INDRIANI

Over the years, mobile phones have grown from being a luxury item into a basic need, due to rapid technological growth and the need to stay connected. And many people have taken advantage of this mobile phone development to expand business capabilities, to network, and to increase quality of life. Business was heavily influenced by this global change, adjusting to the high increase in mobile phone usage.

Mobile phone users in Indonesia now number over 250 million people (Nugraha, 2012). Most of these people use their mobile phones religiously, carrying it almost all the time and checking for messages regularly (Wardhana, 2012). Therefore, mobile phone marketing was considered an effective way to market products or services. But past studies show a contrasting result: People are not interested with mobile phone marketing for reasons such as insecurity and unreliable service.

Given the fact that mobile phone use in Indonesia is growing even more prevalent (Yoga, 2012), the big question is why mobile phone marketing still does not attract consumers effectively. This study explores the differences in mobile phone marketing perspectives among different demographic groups in Indonesia and the reasons for those differences.

Conceptualization

A previous study by Nysveen and Pedersen (2005) is used as the main foundation for this conceptual framework, where knowledge, risk, and experience are three main factors that affect the intention to purchase products. To construct a new framework for this study, "trust," based on Basheer and Ibrahim (2010), and "acceptance," based from Gao, Sultan, and Rohm (2010), are added to the framework.

Methodology

For this research, measurements were derived from previous research articles (as shown in Table 15.1). Almost all those measures were first converted, adjusted, and validated based on given situations in Indonesia. The research was conducted in Indonesia, covering three cities: Bandung, Jakarta, and Purwokerto. Judgmental sampling is used in this research, meaning that the researcher chooses the sample based on who would be the most suitable and appropriate for this study after consulting with the expert in the field. Anyone who has ever received mobile phone marketing through SMS (short messaging service) is considered a valid respondent.

Findings and Results

Validation and Reliability

The Cronbach's alpha value for most of whole item is valid, meaning that the instrument has a high level of consistency (above 0.6), as suggested by Hair et al. (2006), except for mobile phone marketing that shows unsatisfactory internal satisfactory reliability. All variables have a Kaiser-Meyer-Olkin (KMO) value above 0.5, and the total variance extracted is also higher than 50 percent, showing that construct validity is achieved (see Table 15.2).

Based on previous research conducted by the Pew Research Center and further observations conducted in Indonesia, people

Table 15.1

Measures Used in This Study

Variables	Source and Measurement	Scaling Method
Mobile phone marketing risk	Chaudhuri (2000)	Six-scale Likert
Mobile phone marketing knowledge	Smith and Park (1980), Mitchell and Dacin (1996)	Six-scale Likert
Perceived usefulness	Davis et al. (1989)	Six-scale Likert
Perceived ease of use	Davis et al. (1989)	Six-scale Likert
Compatibility	Moore and Benbasat (1991)	Six-scale Likert
Attitude toward mobile phone marketing	Ajzen and Fishbein (1980)	Six-scale Likert
Trust	Swan et al. (1988), Delgado-Ballester and Munuera Aleman (2005)	Six-scale Likert
Mobile phone marketing acceptance	Barwise and Strong (2002)	Six-scale Likert
Mobile phone marketing experience	Bruner and Kumar (2000), Nysveen and Pedersen (2002)	Six-scale Likert
Intention to purchase product	Ang et al. (2001), Han et al. (2008), Park et al. (2008)	Six-scale Likert

in 17–25 years age range tend to use mobile phones intensively, hence their involvement level becomes very high. As a result, their understanding of mobile phone marketing is considered better than it is for other age ranges. Almost 95 percent of more than 400 respondents for this research are 17–25 years old, which is an excellent representation of active users of mobile phones.

Mobile phone usage is growing due to rapid growth in mobile phone technology and social media applications. Students, in this case, are one of the categories or occupations that are highly involved with mobile phones to support their academic and social activities. Therefore, students in big cities are suitable respondents with regard to mobile phone marketing.

Residence cities are the regions where this research is conducted, or the three cities of Bandung, Jakarta, and Purwokerto. By conducting this research in those three cities, the effect of mobile phone marketing in the capital and rural cities can be distinguished. One hundred and eighty-eight respondents are from Purwokerto (a rural city), Bandung (a capital city of West Java province) had 159 respondents, and Jakarta (the capital city of Indonesia) had 89 respondents. The demographic profile "expense" defines the respondent's economic status. Almost half the respondents spend Rp 1 million (±100 USD) to Rp 2 million (±200 USD) a month with the smallest percentage coming from respondents with expenses of more than Rp 4 million (±400 USD) a month.

Most of the respondents spend less than 10 percent of their monthly income to buy products through mobile phone marketing; 20.5 percent of respondents spend 10–25 percent and the rest, 2.56 percent, spend 26–50 percent of their monthly income to buy products through mobile phone marketing. It indicates that people still have some doubts about mobile phone marketing that prevent them from fully accepting it. The following discussion further describes the reasons for this spending pattern.

The second and also the last behavior profile in this section explain which products are frequently purchased through mobile phone marketing. Options given in the questionnaire include phone credits, electronic devices, tickets (train, airplane, concert, theater, etc.), and automotive. Phone credit is the product most purchased

Table 15.2

Validation and Reliability

Variable	KMO	Total variance explained	Cronbach's alpha reliability
Mobile phone marketing risk	0.522	51.719	0.548
Mobile phone marketing knowledge	0.644	68.287	0.758
Trust	0.868	62.912	0.881
Mobile phone marketing acceptance	0.67	64.912	0.729
Mobile phone marketing experience	0.779	50.473	0.751
Intention to purchase product	0.744	58.335	0.751

through mobile phone marketing (63.5 percent). If we compare phone credit with the other products, phone credits are not physical products, and therefore people do not have to worry about defective products or other risks associated with physical products. While 17.16 percent of the respondents never buy anything through mobile phone marketing for personal reasons, such as that they consider the message only as information, it is not a motivation to buy the product. However, it can be determined that almost all the respondents have received mobile phone marketing even though some of them might have formed bad impressions about it.

Demographic Differences in Mobile Phone Marketing in Indonesia

Table 15.3 shows the relationship between ordinal-type data of demographic profiles with behavioral profiles. There is a relationship between age and electronic devices and tickets, as the products bought through mobile phone marketing, and a relationship between monthly income and mobile phone marketing shopping expenses, electronic devices, tickets, and other products.

Age and expense are not significantly related to phone credit buying, probably because all respondents, regardless of their age, are buying phone credit just like other people. So age is not an appropriate criterion to indicate phone credit buying. As for the expense, phone credits are available in many packages, from Rp 5,000 to Rp 100,000 (0.5 USD–10 USD), so people will easily buy based

Table 15.3

Result of Crosstab Ordinal-Typed Data with Behavioral Profiles

	Mobile Phone Marketing Shopping Expense (%)		Product Bought									
			Phone credit		Electronic device		Ticket		Automotive		Never		Others	
	Kendall's	Sig.	Kendall's	Sig.	Kendall's	Sig.	Kendall's	Sig.	Kendall's	Sig.	Kendall's	Sig.	Kendall's	Sig.
Age	−0.041	0.255	−0.073	0.180	−0.027	0.015	−0.047	0.002	−0.018	0.057	0.104	0.073	0.006	0.889
Expense	0.156	0.000	−0.001	0.986	0.112	0.021	0.176	0.001	0.005	0.917	−0.053	0.272	0.125	0.002

on their credit needs and buying power. Selling Automotive is also not significant either with age or expense because it is considered too risky to be bought through mobile phone marketing.

Conceptual Model for Mobile Phone Marketing in Indonesia

Figure 15.1 shows that trust tends to have the biggest impact on the intention to purchase the product followed by mobile phone marketing experience.

Trust consists of six indicators: comfort of purchasing a product offered through mobile phone marketing, purchase frequency, credibility of mobile phone marketing, fulfillment from the seller, guarantee given by the seller, and honesty and sincerity of the seller in addressing buyer's concerns. Respondents' trust of mobile phone marketing is less satisfactory. They slightly disagree on the statements in the questionnaire that generally state that mobile phone marketing can be trusted. Sellers with bad credentials are to blame for this result; they are the reason mobile phone marketing is not as successful in Indonesia as it is in other countries. It makes it even harder to trust because customers cannot see, feel,

Figure 15.1 **Conceptual Model**

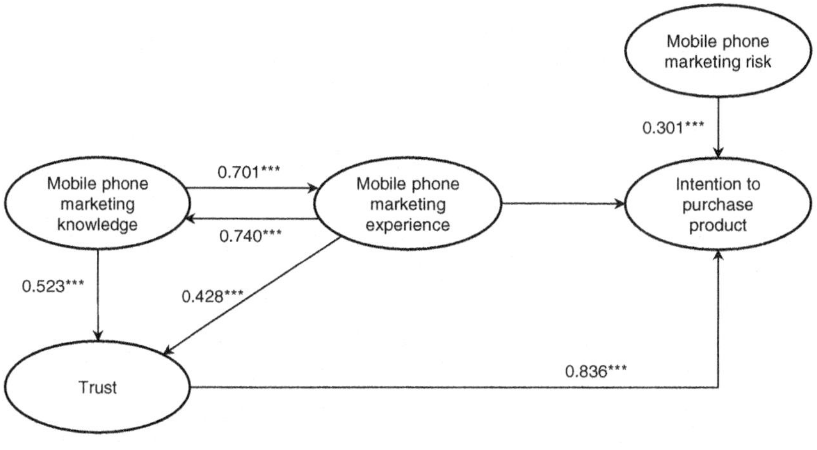

Note: ***$p = 0.000$

or touch the products to see the quality of the product. Moreover, what worries them the most is that there is no official guarantee of a safe transaction. That is why trust must become very fundamental in this buying process.

Mobile phone marketing experience indicators are mobile phone marketing experience, effectiveness of mobile phone marketing as a marketing medium for certain product or service, mobile phone utilization, responsiveness toward mobile phone marketing, and proficiency toward mobile phone marketing. Mobile phone marketing knowledge comes with three indicators: respondents' perception of their knowledge regarding mobile phone marketing, how much knowledge they have with regard to mobile phone marketing, and their expertise in this subject. This means that the more knowledge someone has about mobile phone marketing, the easier for him or her to operate it. For respondents to gain noteworthy experience with mobile phone marketing, they must, first, have good knowledge about it. A good experience leads to a higher intention to purchase products. Gaining better knowledge and trust after a purchase is made will eventually influence the next intention to buy.

Mobile phone risk represents the economic consequences generated from being involved with mobile phone marketing, the quality of the product offered through mobile phone marketing, the possible security risk, and the resulting image as buyer in mobile phone marketing influence intention to purchase, although not as high as trust as influencing factors.

Conclusion

There are pros and cons regarding mobile phone marketing activity in Indonesia. Based on this study, it is safe to say that acceptance of mobile phone marketing in Indonesia is not very high. Some believe that mobile phone marketing is an effective way to market your products or services because the approach is personal and the dissemination process is rapid. On the contrary, customers consider mobile phone marketing less trustworthy, mainly because of fear of low credibility of the seller.

Trust is the main issue in mobile phone marketing usage in Indonesia. The seller must guarantee responsiveness, reliability, and credibility to be able to improve the customer's view of mobile phone marketing.

As for the product bought through mobile phone marketing, people tend to be more amenable to buying a low-involvement product, which needs less consideration, such as phone credits, through mobile phone marketing.

Recommendations

1. Further research can be done to explore the antecedents of trust in mobile phone marketing and explore the reasons for the low trust level among Indonesian customers.
2. The study can offer alternative results when the observation is directed to analyze the ease in using mobile phone technology as a means of transaction.

Implication

The result of this study can be benefit industrial marketing strategy. Mobile phone producers should consider usage of mobile phones as a means of transaction in developing mobile phone applications. The applications should be able to address and eliminate customer's concerns about buying products using mobile phones.

Mobil phone marketing is the recent development in marketing, utilizing advanced technology in mobile phones. Improvement of mobile phone marketing performance in Indonesia should start by increasing customer knowledge and trust of this method of selling. Providing incentives can also be a solution to increase purchase intention to buy products through mobile phones.

References

Ajzen, I., and Fishbein, M. (1980). *Understanding attitudes and predicting social behavior.* Englewood Cliffs, NJ: Prentice-Hall.

Ang, S.H., Cheng, P.S., Lim E.A.C., and Tambyah, S.K. (2001). Spot the difference: Consumer responses towards counterfeits. *Journal of Consumer Marketing,* 18(3), 219–235.

Barwise, P., and Strong, C. (2002). Permission-based mobile advertising. *Journal of Interactive Marketing*, 16(7), 14–24.

Basheer, A.M.A., and Ibrahim, A.M.A. (2010). Mobile marketing: Examining the impact of trust, privacy concern, and consumers' attitudes on intention to purchase. *International Journal of Business and Management*, 5(3), 28–41.

Bruner, G.C., and Kumar, A. (2000). Web commercials and advertising hierarchy of effects. *Journal of Advertising Research*, 40(January/April), 35–42.

Chaudhuri, A. (2000). A macro analysis of the relationship of product involvement and information search: The role of risk. *Journal of Marketing Theory and Practice*, 8(1), 1–16.

Davis, F., Bagozzi, R.P., and Warshaw, P.R. (1989). User acceptance of computer technology: A comparison of two theoretical models. *Management Science*, 35(8), 982–1003.

Delgado-Balesster, E., and Munuera-Aleman, J.L. (2005). Does brand trust matter to brand equity? *Journal of Product and Brand Management*, 14(2/3), 187–196.

Gao, T., Sultan, F., and Rohm, A.J. (2010). Factors influencing Chinese youth consumers' acceptance of mobile phone marketing. *Journal of Consumer Marketing*, 27(7), 574–583.

Hair, J.F., Black, W.C., Babin, B.J., Anderson, R.E., and Tatham, R.L. (2006). *Multivariate data analysis*, 6th ed. Upper Saddle River, NJ: Pearson/Prentice-Hall.

Han, J.M., Suk, H.J., and Chung, K.W. (2008). The influence of logo exposure in purchasing counterfeit luxury goods: Focusing on consumer values. Paper presented at the International DMI Education Conference, ESSEC Business School, Cergy-Pointoise, France.

Mitchell, A.A., and Dacin, P.A. (1996). The assessment of alternative measures of consumer expertise. *Journal of Consumer Research*, 23, 219–239.

Nugraha, B.A. (2012). Pengguna Ponsel di Indonesia. (Cell phone users in Indonesia). www.solopos.com/2012/feature/pengguna-ponsel-di-indonesia-191426 (accessed July 20, 2012).

Nysveen, H., and Pedersen, P.E. (2005). Search mode and purchase intention in online shopping behavior. *International Journal of Internet Marketing and Advertising*, 2(4), 288–306.

Park, H.J., Rabolt, N.J., and Jeon, K.S. (2008). Purchasing global luxury brands among young Korean consumers. *Journal of Fashion Marketing and Management*, 12(2), 244–259.

Smith, D.C., and Park, C.W. (1992). The effect of brand extensions on market share advertising efficiency. *Journal of Marketing Research*, 29, 296–313.

Swan, J.E., Trawick, I.F., Rink, D.R. and Roberts, J.J. (1988). Measuring dimensions of purchaser trust of industrial sales. *Journal of Personal Selling & Sales Management*, 8, 1–9.

Wardhana, A. (2012). Perkiraan Jumlah Pengguna Internet dan Media Sosial di 2012. (Predicted Internet and Social Media Users in 2012), February 18. http://salingsilang.com/baca/perkiraan-jumlah-pengguna-internet-dan-sosial-media-di-2012/ (accessed July 20, 2012).

Yoga. (2012). Pengguna Blackberry Indonesia Akan Naik Hingga 9.7 Juta Pada 2015. (Blackberry Users in Indonesia would rise up to 9.7 M in 2015), May 24. www.jeruknipis.com/node/9403/ (accessed July 20, 2012).

16

Toward a Differentiated Understanding of Social Media Usage and Participation Benefits

A Cross-Cultural Comparison Between Eastern and Western Users

WERNER H. KUNZ AND RAYMOND R. LIU

Today, activities in social media captivate people around the world, and community platforms (e.g., Facebook, QQ, Renren, Twitter) are becoming increasingly important for the marketing strategies of businesses worldwide. Community platforms offer participants a variety of possibilities to promote their own ideas, to communicate with others, and to make use of online content or interactive applications, resulting in completely new consumer behavior (Hennig-Thurau et al., 2010). Because of new media characteristics (e.g., digital, low cost, ubiquity), online communities have become rapidly spreading global phenomena that now attract individuals around the world. For instance, China is becoming a giant Internet and online community market. According to the China Internet Network Information Center (CNNIC, 2013), in December 2012, there were 538 million Internet users in China, and 318 million of them used online communities. Thus, China has already double the number of online community members as in the United States, which manifests China's importance for online community research. Although online communities are a global phenomenon, most empirical research has been conducted in Western countries that are significantly and culturally distinct from Asian countries. Due to these cultural differences, it is not clear whether the results from Western countries also hold true in the Eastern context. Prior research generally has focused on overall online community behavior (Dholakia, Bagozzi, and Pearo, 2004; Foster, Francescucci, and West, 2010; Jahn and Kunz, 2012; Raacke and Bonds-Raacke, 2008), without considering the potential for cultural differences.

This study analyzes the role of various online activities for consumers in their relationship to the community and shows significant cross-cultural differences between Western and Eastern societies. In particular, we focus on the following research questions: What are the main online activities on community platforms? How does the type of activity on community platforms influence the members' online experiences and online community loyalty? What kinds of behavioral differences exist between Western and Eastern community participants? To answer these questions, we have developed a taxonomy of online community activities and a framework of online community behavior based on functional and hedonic theory value (Hirschman and Holbrook, 1982), cross-cultural models (Hofstede, 1980; Markus and Kitayama, 1991; Zhang, Beatty, and Walsh, 2008), and Confucian philosophy (Riegel, 2006; Vuylsteke et al., 2010).

The taxonomy of online activities including public posting, personal communication, and entertainment. Each of the dimensions encompasses a set of very unique and important online community behaviors that are available in the majority of online communities worldwide (e.g., Facebook, Renren, CyWorld). The three dimensions of the taxonomy have been tested empirically in an online survey according to data from online communities in the United States and China (i.e., focus groups, 203 participants in a qualitative survey, 521 in a quantitative survey) and show cross-cultural stability (i.e., partially measurement invariance; Steenkamp and Baumgartner, 1998).

In the framework development, we follow a basic approach and divide user online behavior process into three zones: activity on the platform (i.e., public posting, personal communication, and entertainment), participation benefit (i.e., rational benefit, emotional benefit), and long-term relationship to the community (i.e., community loyalty). The basic idea of this framework is that, if a member engages in a particular activity on the platform, he or she experiences some kind of benefit from this activity. The degree of the experienced benefit influences the relationship of the user to the online community platform in such a way that he or she becomes more loyal and uses it more regularly. We assume that the described process differs in various countries based on cultural reasons. For instance, rational benefits drive community loyalty more strongly in Eastern-collectivistic societies than in Western-individualistic societies due to the doctrine of the mean (Riegel, 2006). Because Eastern society is more collectivistic, the influence of public posting on participation benefits is stronger in Eastern than in Western societies, while in Western-individualistic societies the influence of personal communication plays a major role.

To test the framework, we generated multi-item scales for the constructs of the framework, on the basis of previous measures, the qualitative pre-studies, and the theoretical foundation. The questions were phrased very generally and did not contain any specific platform that exists only at Facebook or Renren. A cross-cultural study was conducted at two universities in the United States (267 participants) and China (254 participants). SEM multigroup with a maximum likelihood estimator was used to analyze the data. The statistics indicate an adequate fit of the proposed relationships (i.e., $\chi^2/df = 3.7$; CFI = .903; RMSEA= .073).

We found in our study that Chinese participants are more driven by the rational-functional route in their loyalty to the community platform ($\Delta\chi^2 = 7.1$, $\Delta df = 2$, $p < .02$). This is in accordance with previous research and the Confucian philosophy in an Eastern society. Chinese people have an intrinsic tendency to follow the logic of rectitude and moderation (e.g., being rational) and rely less on emotional expression than Americans (Lim and Ang, 2008; Liu and McClure, 2001).

The preference for rational benefits and a harmonious way in social activities can be also observed in Chinese behavior toward entertainment, in particular, games and applications in the online community. While, in the United States, entertainment is perceived as a hedonic activity, purely hedonic consumption would be considered excessive in China. Chinese participants can appreciate the social interaction in the entertainment applications of the online community because it meets their need for social exchange with their peers. From a Western perspective, entertainment applications in online communities in their current form do not offer any rational reasons for participation.

We found that personal communication is more emphasized for Americans and Americans' personal communication behavior leads to stronger rational and emotional benefit than is the case for the Chinese ($\Delta\chi^2 = 6.3$, $\Delta df = 2$, $p < .04$). Public posting of activities is a unique feature of online communities; people from both collectivist and individualist countries are excited about it, which leads to significant outcomes of perceived rational and emotional benefits ($\Delta\chi^2 = 2.61$, $\Delta df = 2$, $p > .27$).

The results of this study emphasize how important it is to consider cross-cultural differences in online community research and that empirical results from one region could lead to misleading implications in regions with different cultural backgrounds (Huff and Smith, 2008).

References

CNNIC. (2013). 30th statistical report on Internet development in China. http://www1.cnnic.cn/IDR/ReportDownloads/201209/t20120928_36586.htm (accessed January 8, 2013).

Dholakia, U.M., Bagozzi, R.P., and Pearo, L.K. (2004). A social influence model of consumer participation in network- and small-group-based virtual communities. *International Journal of Research in Marketing*, 21(3), 241–263.

Foster, M., Francescucci, A., and West, B. (2010). Why users participate in online social networks. *International Journal of e-Business Management*, 4(1), 3–18.

Hennig-Thurau, T., Malthouse, E.C., Friege, C., Gensler, S., Lobschat, L., Rangaswamy, A., and Skiera, B. (2010). The impact of new media on customer relationships. *Journal of Service Research*, 13(3), 311–330.

Hirschman, E.C., and Holbrook, M.B. (1982). Hedonic consumption—Emerging concepts, methods and propositions. *Journal of Marketing*, 46(2), 92–101.

Hofstede, G. (1980). *Culture's consequences: National differences in thinking and organizing*. New York: McGraw-Hill.

Huff, L., and Smith, S. (2008). Cross-cultural business research: Introduction to the special issue. *Journal of Business Research*, 61(3), 179–182.

Jahn, B., and Kunz, W. (2012). How to transform consumers into fans of your brand. *Journal of Service Management,* 23(3), 344–361.

Lim, E., and Ang, S. (2008). Hedonic vs. utilitarian consumption: A cross-cultural perspective based on cultural conditioning. *Journal of Business Research,* 61(3), 225–232.

Liu, R.R., and McClure, P. (2001). Recognizing cross-cultural differences in consumer complaint behavior and intentions: an empirical examination. *Journal of Consumer Marketing,* 18(1), 54–75.

Markus, H., and Kitayama, S. (1991). Culture and the self: Implications for cognition, emotion, and motivation. *Psychological Review,* 98(2), 224–253.

Raacke, J., and Bonds-Raacke, J.B. (2008). MySpace and Facebook: Applying the uses and gratifications theory to exploring friend-networking sites. *CyberPsychology and Behavior,* 11(2), 169–174.

Riegel, J. (2006). Confucius. In E.N. Zalta (Ed.), *The Stanford encyclopedia of philosophy.* Stanford: Stanford University Press.

Steenkamp, J.-B., and Baumgartner, H. (1998). Assessing measurement invariance in cross-national consumer research. *Journal of Consumer Research,* 25(1), 78–91.

Vuylsteke, A., Wen, Z., Baesens, B., and Poelmans, J. (2010). Consumers' search for information on the Internet: How and why China differs from Western Europe. *Journal of Interactive Marketing,* 24(4), 309–331.

Zhang, J., Beatty, S., and Walsh, G. (2008). Review and future directions of cross-cultural consumer services research. *Journal of Business Research,* 61(3), 211–224.

17

Shape Matters

How Logo Shapes Influence Consumer Reactions

YUWEI JIANG, GERALD J. GORN, MARIA GALLI,
AND AMITAVA CHATTOPADHYAY

Brand logos are important components of any company's identity. Previous empirical research on brand logos (e.g., Henderson and Cote 1998; Henderson et al. 2003; Janiszewski and Meyvis 2001) has focused primarily on measures related to its aesthetic appeal (e.g., how beautiful a particular logo is) and on ease of recognition. How different logo shapes influence consumers' perceptions of the company and its products is still largely unknown. This is the focus of our research.

Broadly speaking, logo designs can be classified as angular, circular, or a combination of the two. Angular shapes are those consisting of straight lines and sharp corners (e.g., a rectangle); whereas circular shapes are curved and without sharp angles (e.g., an oval). According to Berlyne (1976), angular shapes induce confrontational associations such as energy, toughness, and strength. In contrast, circular shapes induce compromise associations such as approachableness and friendliness (e.g., Liu and Kennedy 1994). We expect that the associations that a person has with an angular vs. round shape, will transfer to consumers' perceptions of objects with that shape. Regarding brand logos, we expect the associations to transfer to the brand associated with the logo. Specifically, we predict that circular brand logos have a symbolic meaning of "soft," and angular brand logos have a symbolic meaning of "hard" and hence that the symbolic meaning of "soft" and "hard" will influence consumers' perceptions of the brand and its product characteristics. We test this hypothesis in four experiments.

In experiment 1, participants were asked to give us their initial reactions toward a company and its products after viewing either a circular logo or an angular logo. As expected, participants judged the brand using a circular logo to: (1) be less tough/hard than the brand using an angular logo, and (2) more likely to be in an industry associated with softness (e.g., *daycare center* or *pet shop*) than the brand using an angular logo; the brand using an angular logo was perceived to be more likely in an industry associated with toughness (e.g., *construction company* or *law firm*) than the brand using a circular logo.

Several important product attributes are closely connected with the concept of "soft" vs. "hard/tough." Products made of soft materials are usually perceived to be more comfortable to use, for example. In contrast, products made of hard materials are usually perceived to be capable of lasting longer. Thus the second experiment examined whether different logo shapes can influence consumers' beliefs about a product's comfortableness and durability. We also tested whether the observed logo inference effect occurs through a process of misattribution, akin to the "How-do-I-feel-about-it?" heuristic (Schwarz and Clore 1988). After seeing a shoe ad with either a circular or an angular logo, participants were either asked to explicitly report their logo-shape inferences (e.g., "The logo gave me the impression that the shoe is very comfortable/durable") before they reported their beliefs of the comfortableness/durability of the shoe, or to report the shape inferences after reporting their product beliefs. We found that participants believed the product is more comfortable when the brand had a circular logo, and that the product is more durable when the brand has an angular logo. Moreover, consistent with the misattribution hypothesis, the effect of logo shape on product beliefs disappeared when participants were explicitly asked about their logo inferences before measuring their product beliefs.

Experiment 3 built on the first two studies by exploring the relationship between explicit verbal claims and the logo. We examine whether the consistency between the inference drawn from the logo's shape and the verbal claims leads to more favorable outcomes than when the logo shape and verbal claims are not matched. Participants were shown a shoe ad with either a circular or an angular brand logo. Also the verbal information contained in the shoe ad focused either on the comfortableness of the shoe or its durability. Consistent with expectations, the results showed a matching effect. Consumers liked the shoe more and were willing to pay more for the shoe if the logo shape inferences were consistent with the verbal information in the advertisement.

Experiment 4 attempted to expand the generalizability of our findings by showing that brand logo shapes not only influence consumer inferences about specific product attributes, but also inferences about general brand characteristics, including the behavior of company employees. Extending the idea that circular logos lead to inferences of softness to the notion that soft also implies caring, we examined whether consumers expected companies with circular logos to be more responsive to consumer needs. Participants were shown a consumption scenario–a passenger has overweight luggage when trying to board an airplane operated by an airline company with either a circular logo or an angular logo—and asked how likely the passenger was to be allowed to board without some penalty. As expected, participants predicted that the airline company would be more likely to allow the passenger to bring their bag on board without penalty if the company has a circular brand logo. Participants also thought that the airline company was more willing to respond to consumer needs/demands, and cared more about its customers if the brand used a circular logo.

Summarizing, we find that brand logo shapes impact both specific product attribute judgments and overall product evaluations. We show that this impact is due to a misattribution of the inference elicited by the logo shape and that it is stronger when the explicit claims are in line with the inference elicited by the logo, inferences which seem to be outside the consumers' awareness. These findings are novel and contribute to our theoretical understanding of how brand logos can influence consumers' responses to a brand. Our research has practical implications, in suggesting that companies should choose logos that have aesthetic properties that reinforce the desired image of the brand.

References

Berlyne, D.E. (1976). Psychological aesthetics. *International Journal of Psychology,* 11, 43–55.

Henderson, P.W., and Cote, J.A. (1998). Guidelines for selecting or modifying logos. *Journal of Marketing,* 62, 14–30.

Henderson, P.W., Cote, J.A., Leong, S.M., and Schmitt, B. (2003). Building strong brands in Asia: Selecting the visual components of image to maximize brand strength. *International Journal of Research in Marketing,* 20, 297–313.

Janiszewski, C., and Meyvis, T. (2001). Effects of brand logo complexity, repetition, and spacing on processing fluency and judgment. *Journal of Consumer Research,* 28, 18–32.

Liu, C.H., and Kennedy, J.M. (1994). Symbolic forms can be mnemonics for recall. *Psychonomics Bulletin and Review,* 29, 494–498.

Schwarz, N., and Clore, G.L. (1988). How do I feel about it? Informative functions of affective states. In K. Fiedler and J. Forgas (Eds.), *Affect, cognition, and social behavior,* 44–62. Toronto: Hogrefe International.

18

Analyses of Corporate Visual Identities

Reaction of Japanese Consumers to Global Logo Changes

NAOKO MORIYOSHI AND MIHO SASAKI

In the recent past, a number of global companies have gone through corporate visual identity (CVI) changes, such as renewal of logos or product packages. Unfortunately, as has been the case with Tropicana and The GAP, CVI changes often face acute backlash from consumers, resulting in significant financial and brand damage to the corporation. This chapter analyzes Japanese consumers' reactions to global logo changes. Results indicate that both aesthetic and perceptual factors, such as design evaluation and mere-exposure effect, affect the affinity and likability of the CVIs. Data suggest that culture-specific as well as universal orientations of design perception and its effects on purchasing behavior do exist. The present study provides empirical data that support consumers' voice and reactions to changes in global CVIs.

Objective

In October 2010, The Gap launched a new logo. The intention was to revitalize the brand, but the logo was withdrawn after intense backlash from American consumers. PepsiCo Americas Beverages likewise had to discontinue use of its new Tropicana Pure Premium Orange Juice package one month after its rollout in January 2009. The financial cost and damage to the brand from such failures in the United States have been high. This is in stark contrast to the subdued consumer reaction in Japan when familiar logos are redesigned. This chapter explores why the American and Japanese consumers react so differently to the introduction of new logos. The primary focus is on Japanese consumers to investigate their specific versus universal preferences with regard to perceptual stimuli or designs and how such preferences affect consumer reactions to changes in logos or packages and consumers' consequent purchase intention for these products.

Conceptualization

Van der Lans et al. (2009), based on their cross-national logo evaluation analysis, suggested that a standardized core logo could work globally. Other studies (Masuda and Nisbett, 2001; Morris and Peng, 1994; Zhang et al., 2006) assert that cultural differences in perception exist. Masuda and Nisbett have suggested that the perceptual attention of those from the East and the West are different. Asians tend to pay more holistic attention to the background, whereas Westerners pay more focal attention to salient objects. In addition to the cultural factors, individual factors, such as familiarity/fluency with certain designs or mere-exposure effect, can explain individual differences in how visual stimuli are perceived (Bornstein, 1989; Bornstein and D'Agostino, 1992, 1994; Kunst-Wilson and Zajonc, 1980; Zajonc, 1968). In order to understand such intertwined effects of nature and nurture on the perception of visual images, the following hypotheses were tested:

Hypothesis 1: Basic designs, such as a circle, are more likable when they are complete vs. incomplete.
Hypothesis 2: Prior experience or exposure to certain visual stimuli affects affinity and evaluation. Individuals with higher levels of exposure to streets saturated with visual stimuli or those with artistic experience are more receptive to the new.
Hypothesis 3: Higher levels of exposure to a given design can result in higher likability and a higher purchase intention for the products with these designs.

Methodology

In the present study, basic designs, such as a circle, a square, or a double circle, were used to examine whether any universal or culture-specific perceptual preferences or orientations exist. Familiarity with previous designs was also assessed to avoid the confounding effect of the mere-exposure/fluency to certain stimuli.

Method

Participants

A total of 58 university students (56 undergraduates and 2 graduate students; 28 males and 28 females) from the Tokyo metropolitan area whose mother tongue is Japanese voluntarily participated in the study, conducted in January to February 2012. Their ages ranged from 18.8 to 36.0 years (M [means] = 20.8, SD [standard deviation] = 2.5). Participants signed a written consent form prior to the experiment.

Stimuli and Procedures

Participants responded to questions regarding visual stimuli (slides) shown on an eye-tracker (Tobii T60) screen for about 15 minutes, followed by a 15-minute questionnaire.

The eye tracker recorded the eye movements of the respondents while they were engaged in Tasks 1–4 (total of 122 slides). In Task 1 (12 slides), the images shown to them were circles of various degrees of completeness (from 30° to 360° with 30° × 12 increments). It tested change-blindness, which measures how sensitive an individual is to gradual changes. Task 2 (47 slides) asked the respondents whether they thought the image was enclosed. Four designs (circle in solid line, circle in dots, square in dots, and a mountain inside a dotted circle) that varied in the degree of enclosure (from 1 percent to 100 percent) were presented (see Figure 18.1 for examples).

Task 3 (53 slides) asked the respondents regarding the likability of each image, which varied in its completeness/enclosure or alignment/position. Various images of seven designs (enclosed mountain, double circles, circle with square, ECN, APG, partial

Figure 18.1 **Task 2 Design Examples**

Figure 18.2 **Task 4 Example**

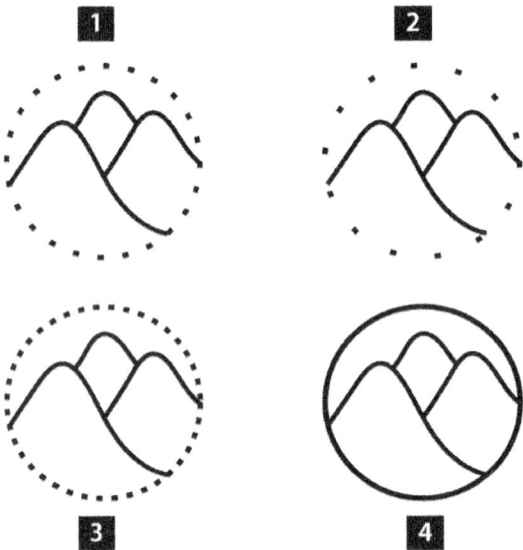

sun, and whole sun) were rated on a Likert-type scale from 1 (very likable) to 6 (very unlikable). Task 4 consisted of 10 slides with 4 images in one slide (top left, top right, bottom left, bottom right) (see Figure 18.2).

Respondents were asked which image they liked the most out of the four shown in the same slide. The images used in Task 4 were selected from those used in Tasks 1–3 to examine the interrater reliability and most likable designs.

Throughout the tasks, participants were asked to respond as quickly as possible, moving to the next slide upon completion of the previous task. All the stimulus exposures were approximately 1 second apart, preceded by a 1-second blank slide with a fixation point (+) in the center. The order of the slide presentation in each task was randomized by the eye tracker for each respondent to control the order effect.

The questionnaire included questions regarding the participants' demographic/personal background information, prior experience in art/design training, familiarity with selected stimuli (photos of six logos + old and new Starbucks logos) and affinity with/evaluation of them. The six logos presented in the questionnaire were (1) Arm and Hammer, (2) Espresso Café, (3) Gap (old and current), (4) Gap (defunct version launched in 2010), (5) Starbucks (old), and (6) Starbucks (new). The order of the logo presentation was randomized for each respondent. Respondents were asked to rate familiarity, evaluation, and likability of the logos on a Likert-type scale from 1 to 6 ("Not familiar at all" to "Very familiar," "Not good at all" to "Very good," and "Very likable" to "Very unlikable"). For the Starbucks old and new logos, participants were asked to rate frequency of the visit to the stores and preference of the logo (new or old) on a Likert-type scale from 1 to 6 ("Prefer the old logo very much" to "Prefer the new logo very much"). To test H2, previous exposure to streets with varying degrees of saturation of visual stimuli, such as store signs and boards were assessed based on a photo-rating scale (six photos indicated differing degrees of saturation with visual stimuli from 1 = No stimuli to 6 = Very busy). Purchase intentions for the drinks with fictitious logos or package types were also measured using a Likert-type scale from 1 to 6 ("Not at all" to "Very much so").

Results

All the hypotheses were supported with significant differences. Some gender differences were observed. Females appeared to have a stricter criterion for determining whether the image shown to them was complete or enclosed, especially when semicomplete/enclosed designs were used, such as a 300° or a 330° circle. When viewing such circles, females responded "No, it's not a circle" significantly more often than males ($t(56) = 2.71, p < .01$ and $t(56) = 2.91, p < .01$, respectively).

Table 18.1

Task1_Single Circle: "Is this a circle?" Yes = 1, No = 2

Completeness	Mean	N	SD	SE	
@1_1 (30°)	1.97	58	.184	.024	
@1_2 (60°)	1.95	58	.223	.029	
@1_3 (90°)	1.95	58	.223	.029	
@1_4 (120°)	1.93	58	.256	.034	
@1_5 (150°)	1.97	58	.184	.024	
@1_6 (180°)	1.95	58	.223	.029	
@1_7 (210°)	1.90	58	.307	.040	
@1_8 (240°)	1.83	58	.381	.050	
@1_9 (270°)	1.36	58	.485	.064	
@1_10 (300°)	1.71	58	.459	.060	
@1_11 (330°)	1.66	58	.479	.063	(a)
@1_12 (360°)	1.00	58	.000	.000	

Note: $p = .000$ ($p < .001$) at line (a).

Regarding H1, overall judgments of the images (e.g., whether circles are complete/enclosed) by the respondents indicated that they distinguish incomplete/semicomplete images from complete ones at significant levels and the likability of the images with higher degrees of completeness were rated with lower scores (toward more likable) on the likability rating scales at significant levels. Respondents indicated higher likability, if the image of the circle was completely enclosed in terms of both the images of simple shapes and logos ($r = .501, p < .01$).

For the Task 1 the question "Is this a circle?" a significant division between "yes" and "no" was observed between the 330° and 360° circles. The mean response scores for the 330° and 360° circles were 1.66 (toward No) and 1.00 (Yes), respectively ($t = 10.41(57)$, $p < .001$) (see Table 18.1).

A similar tendency was found in the responses (yes/no) to the Task 2 question, "Is it enclosed?" Table 18.2 gives an overview of the mean response scores for the "Enclosed Mountain" images that differed in the degree of the outer-circle enclosure from 5 percent (dotted) to 100 percent (solid line). Two significant borderlines between the mean scores were found: (1) between 70 percent and 80 percent ($t(57) = 5.72, p < .001$) and (2) between 80 percent and 90

Table 18.2

Task2_Enclosed Mountain: "Is it enclosed?" Yes = 1, No = 2

Degree of Enclosure	Mean	N	SD	SE	
@2_25 (05%) = 3_1	1.88	58	.329	.043	
@2_26 (10%) = 3_2	1.90	58	.307	.040	
@2_27 (20%) = 3_3	1.79	58	.409	.054	
@2_28 (30%) = 3_4	1.72	58	.451	.059	
@2_29 (40%) = 3_5	1.67	58	.473	.062	
@2_30 (50%) = 3_6	1.60	58	.493	.065	
@2_31 (60%) = 3_7	1.57	58	.500	.066	
@2_32 (70%) = 3_8	1.59	58	.497	.065	(a)
@2_33 (80%) = 3_9	1.19	58	.395	.052	(b)
@2_34 (90%) = 3_10	1.05	58	.223	.029	
@2_35 (100%) = 3_11	1.03	58	.184	.024	
@3_11	2.57	58	1.244	.163	

Note: $p = .000$ ($p < .001$) at line (a); $p = .01$ ($p < .05$) at line (b).

percent ($t (57) = 2.66$, $p < .05$). These judgment orientations toward enclosed shapes were also observed in the likability measurements of these images in the Task 3. Table 18.3 summarizes the likability ratings of the same images used in the Task 2. Likability was rated on a scale from 1 to 6 ("Very likable" to "Very unlikable"). Images with relatively lower enclosure rates, 5 percent to 70 percent, received ratings toward "unlikable (Mean scores above 3)," whereas images with higher enclosure rates, 80 percent to 100 percent, received ratings toward "likable (Mean scores below 3)" with two significant borderlines identical to the ones found in the Task 2 results: (1) between 70 percent and 80 percent ($t (57) = 3.60$, $p < .01$) and (2) between 80 percent and 90 percent ($t (57) = 4.04$, $p < .001$).

This tendency to favor enclosed images was also found in evaluating logo designs of single circles and doughnut-shaped double circles used in the old Starbucks logo image. Fictitious doughnut logos with double (inner and outer) edges with white lines were preferred to single (inner or outer only) edged logos or logos with no edges. A significant positive correlation was also found between the likability and the degree of the enclosure of the images used in Tasks 2 and 3 ($r = .301$, $p < .05$). The more enclosed the image was, the more likable the image was.

Table 18.3

Enclosed Mountain: 1 = Very Likable, 6 = Very Unlikable

	Mean	N	SD	SE	
@3_1 (5%)	3.95	58	1.176	.154	
@3_2 (10%)	3.84	58	1.136	.149	
@3_3 (20%)	3.72	58	1.056	.139	
@3_4 (30%)	3.55	58	1.079	.142	
@3_5 (40%)	3.64	58	1.165	.153	
@3_6 (50%)	3.53	58	1.112	.146	(a)
@3_7 (60%)	3.38	58	1.197	.157	(b)
@3_8 (70%)	3.29	58	1.311	.172	
@3_9 (80%)	2.93	58	1.197	.157	
@3_10 (90%)	2.53	58	1.246	.164	
@3_11 (100%)	2.57	58	1.244	.163	

Note: $p = .001$ ($p < .01$) at line (a); $p = .000$ ($p < .001$) at line (b).

Task 4, which asked respondents to choose the most likable design out of the four, presented together on the screen at a time, yielded similar results, supporting the higher likability of the enclosed designs.

Thus, H1 was supported with significant differences suggesting that basic designs, such as a circle or double circle, are liked more when they are complete or enclosed.

Regarding H2, correlation analyses indicate a positive association between the degrees of exposure to busy city signs, such as store signs or boards and the evaluation of unfamiliar designs ($r = .302, p < .05$) as well as a positive association between the degrees of exposure to busy city signs and the degrees of exposure to the new Starbucks logo design ($r = .268, p < .05$). Significant positive correlations were also found between the degrees of the exposure to/familiarity with the Starbucks new logo design and the likability or evaluation of the new logo ($r = .462, p < .01$ and $r = .455, p < .01$, respectively).

Significantly positive correlations were also found between the degrees of experience in artistic work or training/education and the degrees of the likability or evaluation of the Starbucks new logo ($r = .288, p < .05$ and $r = .299, p < .05$, respectively). Similarly, a positive correlation was found between the degrees of experience in artistic work or training/education and the evaluation of unfamiliar logo designs ($r = .302, p < .05$). Results suggest that higher levels of exposure to busy signs or unfamiliar designs could serve to buffer the resistance toward design changes, thus, H2 is supported.

Lastly, for H3, higher levels of exposure to the old and new Starbucks logos were measured by the familiarity or frequency of exposure to the logos on six-point scales. Correlation analyses indicate a significant positive correlation between the degree of likability of the old logo and the degree of the purchase intention of a drink with the old logo design on the package ($r = .519, p < .01$). Positive correlations were also found between the familiarity and the likability of the old logo ($r = .281, p < .05$) and between the familiarity and the overall evaluation of the old logo ($r = .260, p < .05$).

The results also suggest that the basic design preference affected their purchase intentions. In accordance with the observed propensity to favor complete/enclosed designs, participants were more likely to indicate higher purchase intentions for drinks with an edged doughnut logo rather than a logo with a partial edge or no edge (see Table 18.4). Significantly dividing borders were found in the degree of purchase intentions between the drinks with new and old logo designs. Highest purchase intention (4.621 out of 6) was associated with the package with an old Starbucks (with the Trettia name) logo design (#4) followed by with an old Starbucks logo design lacking the outer edge (#3). A fictitious brand name, Trettia, was used to bring respondents' attention to the fictitious logo designs, which varied in the degree of enclosure/boundary (see Figure 18.3).

The likability and evaluation of the Gap logo (current versus defunct) were also analyzed. There was a positive correlation between the likability of enclosed designs and the evaluation of the current Gap logo. Female respondents scored higher on the likability scale and gave a more positive evaluation of the current Gap logo ($r = .288, p < .05$), which could be explained by their stronger preference for enclosed shapes.

The findings in this study suggest that affinity for certain logo designs, such as enclosed shapes, as well as familiarity, could be critical factors in influencing consumer behavior. Thus H3 was supported.

Table 18.4

Purchase Intentions for Each Drink on a 6-Point Scale (1 = Not likely at all to purchase, 6 = Very likely to purchase)

	Post-hoc *t*-tests	Mean (1–6)	SD	SE	*t*	*N*	*p*
Pair 1–2	(1) New with no edge	3.379	.9029	.1677	–.441	28	.663
	(2) New with outer edge	3.448	.9482	.1761			
Pair 1–3	(1) New with no edge	3.379	.9029	.1677	–4.006	28	.000
	(3) Old with no outer edge	4.310	1.0387	.1929			
Pair 1–4	(1) New with no edge	3.379	.9029	.1677	–4.312	28	.000
	(4) Old with edges	4.621	1.1776	.2187			
Pair 2–3	(2) New with outer edge	3.448	.9482	.1761	–3.727	28	.001
	(3) Old with no outer edge	4.310	1.0387	.1929			
Pair 2–4	(2) New with outer edge	3.448	.9482	.1761	–4.627	28	.000
	(4) Old with edges	4.621	1.1776	.2187			
Pair 3–4	(3) Old with no outer edge	4.310	1.0387	.1929	–1.967	28	.059
	(4) Old with edges	4.621	1.1776	.2187			

Figure 18.3 **Differing Starbucks Logos**

1 = New Starbucks logo design with no edge or boundary
2 = New Starbucks logo design with outer edge
3 = Old Starbucks logo design without outer edge
4 = Old Starbucks logo design with both outer and inner edges

Discussion

The results for H1 indicate that some universal design elements are preferred over others. Complete and enclosed images were rated significantly higher than incomplete or semi-enclosed images. Such preference was carried over in judging logo designs that embraced the basic elements, such as enclosed circles or double circles. The old Starbucks logo design was rated as being more likable than the new one because the old one was enclosed, with outer and inner double edges.

The familiarity with design also affected affinity with and evaluation of the designs. Results indicated that the familiarity could be a significant factor in judgment. However, individuals with higher exposure to busy city signs were found to be more receptive to new stimuli or unfamiliar designs. Such individual differences should not be discredited.

The results for purchase intentions for products with varying logo designs indicated that familiarity with or likability of the package design can significantly affect consumers' purchase behavior. The respondents were more willing to purchase the products with their favorite logo designs.

Thus, for businesses to succeed in the global market, both universal aesthetic elements and individual differences, such as varying levels of exposure to certain stimuli, should be taken into account when a logo change is considered.

Acknowledgments

The authors acknowledge a grant from the Keio University Research Fund, which supported the present study. They also acknowledge Yoshiyuki Inaba, who designed the images used in the experiment.

References

Bornstein, R.F. (1989). Exposure and affect: Overview and meta-analysis of research. *Psychological Bulletin,* 106(2), 265–289.
Bornstein, R.F., and D'Agostino, P.R. (1992). Stimulus recognition and the mere exposure effect. *Journal of Personality and Social Psychology,* 63(4), 545–552.
———. (1994). The attribution and discounting of perceptual fluency: Preliminary tests of a perceptual fluency/attributional model of the mere exposure effect. *Social Cognition,* 12(2), 103–128.
Kunst-Wilson, W.R., and Zajonc, R.B. (1980). Affective discrimination of stimuli that cannot be recognized. *Science,* 207, 557–558.
Masuda, T., and Nisbett, R.E. (2001). Attending holistically versus analytically: Comparing the context sensitivity of Japanese and Americans. *Journal of Personality and Social Psychology,* 81(5), 922–934.
Morris, M.W., and Peng, K. (1994). Culture and cause: American and Chinese attributions for social and physical events. *Journal of Personality and Social Psychology,* 67(6), 949–971.
Van der Lans, R., et al. (2009). Cross-national logo evaluation analysis: An individual-level approach. *Marketing Science,* 28(5), 968–985.
Zajonc, R.B. (1968). Attitudinal effects of mere exposure. *Journal of Personality and Social Psychology,* 9(2), 1–27.
Zhang, Y., Feick, L., and Price, L.J. (2006). The impact of self-construal on aesthetic preference for angular versus rounded shapes. *Personality and Social Psychology Bulletin,* 32(6), 794–805.

19

Epilogue

The four parts of this book have presented the psychology of the Asian consumer by focusing on theoretical, cross-cultural, Asia-specific, and practical issues. The authors have covered a wide range of topics of theoretical and conceptual relevance to the study of Asian consumers, including cultural identity, values, family decision making, and goal setting, and a rich array of methodologies, including experiments, surveys, and quantitative modeling. The research featured here is informative for managers regarding practical issues, such as fakes and counterfeits, logo design, and social and mobile media.

As we argued in the beginning, beyond the practical relevance of the topic, the Asian consumer is a relatively new research domain that can be used to test and revise existing theories. Moreover, several research streams have already emerged. The chapters in this book have contributed new frameworks and findings to these prior themes.

Assessing the contributions of the chapters in this book, it is clear that cross-cultural "East–West" comparisons as well as studies in individual Asian consumer markets constitute the vast majority of work done on the Asian consumer. As we pointed out in our introductory chapters, we believe that the most promising approach to achieve a more in-depth understanding of the topic is within-Asia comparisons that allow for examining the similarities and differences among Asian consumers in this economically, socially, and culturally diverse part of the world. Only such research can tell us whether there is "one Asian consumer type," so to speak, or many. Only such research can help us decide whether East–West comparisons are justified by focusing on randomly picked locations in the East (and West). And only such research can tell us whether a focus on a single group of consumers in one country would allow generalizations to other Asian markets and consumers.

Beyond more complex research designs to examine similarities and differences among Asian consumers, we believe that the research domain of "Asian consumers" can also benefit from having researchers focus on unique Asian phenomena and develop new theories to explain them. Such an endeavor promises to be more influential than replications of existing phenomena and findings and can help move the field forward.

We look forward to seeing such research contributions and others relevant to Asian consumers at future conferences and in future publications.

Index

Italic page references indicate figures and tables.

Adolescent yearning for global culture, 90–91
Advertising
  deceptive, 46, 59–62
  mixed emotional appeals in, 16–17
Affective experiences of Asian consumers, 16–18
Agrawal, J., 67
Alcohol consumption data, 18
Amaral, Nelson, 46
Amplification effect, 34–36
Analysis of variance (ANOVA), 93
Analytical thinking, 10
Angular logos, 117, 135–137
Anholt-Gfk Roper national brand indexes (NBI), 67, 70
Asian consumers. *See also* Asian-specific issues; Cross-cultural issues; Practical issues; Theoretical issues
  affective experiences of, 16–18
  beliefs of, 14–16, 45, 47–50
  biculturalism and, 13–14
  consumer psychology and, understanding, 18–19
  counterfeit products and, 56–57
  cross-cultural comparisons among, 6–7, 151–152
  fatalistic beliefs and, 14–16
  force of, growing, 3–4
  future research on, 152
  holistic thinking and, 10–11, 55, 57
  impulsive behavior and, 18
  influence of, growing, 4
  lay beliefs and, 15–16

Asian consumers *(continued)*
  mixed emotional appeals in advertising and, 16–17
  processing information and, 10
  reasons for researching, 5–7
  "saving face" social value and, 14–15
  self-brand connection and, 94–95
  Singapore conference discussing (2012), 7
  surprise gifts and, 17–18
  Western brands and, 16
  worlds of, environmental and contextual, 5–7
Asian Development Bank study (2011), 4
Asian-specific issues
  overview of, 63–64, 151
  Singapore-U.S. social values, 64, 103–113
  South Korean brand connections, 64, 89–95
  Thai consumer preferences, 63–64, 65–85
  Vietnamese household economic decision making, 64, 97–100
Attainment goals, 46, 51–54
Ayurvedic medicine, Asian consumers' beliefs about, 15

Basheer, A.M.A., 120
Beliefs
  of Asian consumers, 14–16, 45, 47–50
  fatalistic, 14–16

153

Beliefs *(continued)*
  lay, 15–16
  in luck, 45, 47–50
Berlyne, D.E., 135
Bettman, J.R., 90
Bias, defensive, 59–62
Bicultural identity integration (BII), 13
Biculturalism, 13–14
Bilingualism, 13–14
Brands. *See also* Corporate visual identities (CVI) and Japanese consumers
  consumer life and cultural influence of, 93–94
  episode, personal, 91–94
  global, 94–95
  logo shape design and, 117, 135–137
  perception of, 11
  Western, 16
Briley, Donnel, 45

Carmon, Ziv, 23
Caucasian consumers, 49, 55–57
Chan, Steven, 46
Chao, P., 66–67
Chattopadhyay, Amitava, 45–46, 117
China
  economy of, 3–4
  growth of, 3
  indigenization of foreign cultures in, fear of, 66
  Internet behavior in, 117, 129–132
  one-child policy in, 6
  per capita income in, 4
  Western brands and consumers in, 16
China Internet Network Information Center (CNNIC), 129
Chinese medicine, Asian consumers' beliefs about, 15
Cho, Sunmyoung, 64
Circular logos, 117, 135–137
Cognitive style, 31–32, 57, 59–60

Collectivist cultures, 10, 12–15, 45–46, 59–60
Connection, defining, 89, 94. *See also* Self-brand connection
Consistent Akaike Information Criterion (CAIC), 84
Consumer decision making. *See also* Corporate visual identities (CVI) and Japanese consumers
  affective experiences and, 16–18
  impulsive behavior and, 24, 41–44
  nation equity and, 68
  self-construal and, 12–13
  social values and, 103–104
Consumer life, cultural influence of brands on, 93–94
Consumer preferences. *See* Thai consumer preferences
Consumer psychology
  Asian consumers and understanding, 18–19
  counterfeit products and, research on, 58
  culture and, 9, 45
  "eighth sin" of, 7
  research themes on Asian consumers and understanding, 18–19
  "Seven Sins of," 7
Corporate visual identities (CVI) and Japanese consumers, study on
  conceptualizaton of, 140
  discussion of, 149–150
  gender differences and, 143
  hypotheses of, 140
  methodology of, 141–143, *142*
  objective of, 139–140
  overview of, 117–118, 139
  results of, 143–147, *144, 145, 146, 148, 149*
  task design example and, 141, *142*
Counterfeit products, 46, 55–58
Country-of-origin effects, 63, 66–68, 84, 90
Cronbach's alpha value, 120

Cross-cultural comparisons, 6–7, 45, 151–152. *See also* Singapore-U.S. social values
Cross-cultural issues. *See also* Culture
  within Asia versus East-West comparisons, 6–7
  counterfeit products, 46, 55–58
  deceptive advertising, 46, 59–62
  goal-directed behavior, 45–46, 51–54
  overview of, 45–46, 151
  risk-taking behavior, 45, 47–50
Cross-sectional study. *See* Singapore-U.S. social values
Cultural dimensions, 10–14
Cultural identity, 47
Cultural liberty, 65–69
Cultural psychology, 10, 14, 58–60
Cultural values, 51–52
Culture. *See also* Cross-cultural issues
  Asian, variations in, 63
  collectivist, 10, 12–15, 45–46, 59–60
  consumer psychology and, 9, 45
  counterfeit products and, 55–58
  deceptive advertising and, 59–62
  dimensions of, 10–14
  global, adolescent yearning for, 90–91
  globalization of, 65–66
  goal-directed behavior and, 45–46, 51–54
  impulse buying and, 42–44
  impulsive behavior and, 41–44
  indigenization of foreign, fear of, 65–66
  individualistic, 10, 12, 14, 45–46, 63
  lay beliefs and, 15–16
  nation competency and, dimension of, 70, *71*
  neural wiring and, 14
  values, beliefs, and meanings and, 14–16, 49

Culture-of-brand origin, 89–90, 93
"Cuteness" concept, 6

Dalton, Amy, 23
Darke, Peter, 45–46, 59
Deceptive advertising, 46, 59–62
Decision making. *See* Asian consumer decision making; Consumer decision making; Economic decision making in Vietnamese households; Corporate visual identities (CVI) and Japanese consumers
Defensive bias, 59–62
Deliberate behavior, 24
Dhar, Ravi, 23
Dholakia, U.M., 42–43
Dialectical Self Scale (DSS), 57
Dialectical thinking, 57
Diary study, 64, 97–100
Dynamic of Global Culture and Its Effects on Thailand's Culture and Society study (2009), 69

East Asia's economy, growth of, 3–4, 9. *See also specific consumer and country*
East-West consumer comparisons, 6–7, 151–152
Economic decision making in Vietnamese households, 64, 97–100
"Eighth sin" of consumer psychology, 7
Emotional appeals in advertising, mixed, 16–17
Escalas, J.E., 90
Estimating model, 70, *71*, 72, 72
Exports, 66, 70, *71*, 77
External contextual information, 30
External locus of control, 45, 47–50

Fatalistic beliefs, 14–16
Field dependence, 30
Freud, Sigmund, 25

Gaklli, Maria, 117
Gao, T., 120
Gap, The, logo changes, 139, 147
Gardner, D.M., 59
General theories, 5–7
Geographic marketing, 104
"Ghost-shift" products, 46, 56–58
Global brands, 94–95. *See also*
 South Korean brand
 connections
Goal-directed behavior
 amplification effect and, 34–36
 attainment goals and, 46, 51–54
 conceptualization and, 33–36
 culture and, 45–46, 51–54
 "if-then" format and, 33
 maintenance goals and, 46, 51–54
 motivation and, 33–36
 planning and, 23–24, 33–37, *36,
  37, 38*
 prevention focused, 10, 35–37, *36,
  37, 38*
 promotion-focused, 10, 35–37, *36,
  37, 38*
 substitution effect and, 34–35
Good luck, belief in, 45, 47–50
Goodenough, D.R., 30
Gorn, Gerald, 117
Governance as dimension of nation
 competency, 70, *71*
Gross Domestic Product (GDP), 65
Gurel-Atay, E., 105
Gurhan-Canli, Z., 67

Hair, J.F., 120
Heine, S.J., 47–48
Heterogeneity in Asian consumer
 decision making, 68–69, 74–75
Hofstede, Geert, 10, 14
Holistic thinking, 10–11, 55, 57
Hong, J., 17
Hong Kong University of Science
 and Technology (HKUST)
 students, identity-linking study
 and, 26–27
Hong, S.-T., 67

Hong, Y.Y., 13
Huang, Li, 23

Ibrahim, A.M.A., 120
Identity-linked promotions, 23,
 25–26
Immigration and investment
 as dimensions of nation
 competency, 70, *71*
Imports, 65
Impulse buying (IB), 24, 41–44
Impulsive behavior
 Asian consumers and, 18
 consumer decision making and, 24,
  41–44
 culture and, 41–44
 deliberate behavior versus, 24
 dimensions of, 41–44
 triggers of, 41
In-group price fairness, 15
Inaba, Yoshiyuki, 150
Independence social value, 51–54
Independent self-construal, 10–13,
 18, 60, 63
Indigenization of foreign cultures,
 fear of, 65–66
Individualistic cultures, 10, 12, 14,
 45–46, 63
Indonesia. *See* Mobile phone
 marketing in Indonesia
"Influence bookkeeping" models,
 100
Institute on Asian Consumer Insight
 (IACI), 63
Interdependence social value, 51–54
Interdependent self-construal, 10–
 13, 18, 60
Internal contextual information, 30
Internal locus of control, 45, 47–50
Internet behavior of Eastern vs.
 Western users, 117, 129–132

Japanese consumers and corporate
 visual identities, study on
 conceptualization of, 140
 discussion of, 149–150

Japanese consumers and corporate visual identities, study on *(continued)*
  gender differences and, 143
  hypotheses of, 140
  methodology of, 141–143, *142*
  objective of, 139–140
  overview of, 117–118, 139
  results of, 143–147, *144, 145, 146, 148, 149*
  task design examples and, 141–147, *142, 144, 145, 146*
Jiang, Yuwei, 117
Jindahra, Pavitra, 63–64

Kahle, Lynn, 64
Kaiser-Meyer-Olkin (KMO) value, 120, *123*
Kamakura, W.A., 67, 77
Kawaii ("cuteness" concept), 6
Keio University Research Fund, 150
Kirchler, Erich, 64
Kitayama, Shinobu, 14
Korean wave (K-Wave), 66, 85
Kunz, Werner, 117

Lay beliefs of Asian consumers, 15–16
Lee, A.Y., 17
Lee, Leonard, 7
Lehman, D.R., 47–48
List of Values, 105, *106*
Liu, Raymond, 117
Logo changes. *See also* Corporate visual identities (CVI) and Japanese consumers
  complete/enclosed vs. semi-enclosed designs and, 141–147, *142, 144, 145, 146, 148,* 149
  considerations for, 149–150
  Gap, The, 139, 147
  Starbucks, 146–147, *148, 149*
  Tropicana Pure Premium Orange Juice, 139
Logo shape designs, 117, 135–137

Longitudinal diary approach, 64, 97–100
Luck, belief in good, 45, 47–50
Lynam, D.R., 41

Maheswaran, D., 67
Maintenance goals, 46, 51–54
Marketing, geographic, 104
Marketing mix, self-construal impact on, 10–14
Marketing promotions, 12
"Means-end chain" research, 103
Memory repression, 23, 25–27
Misleading advertising, 46, 59–62
Mixed emotional appeals in advertising, 16–17
Mixed logit model, 68, 73–77, *78–79*, 81, *82–83*, 84
Mixture of nested logit and mixed logit models, 76–77, *78–79*, 81, *82–83*, 84
Mobile phone marketing in Indonesia
  acceptance and, 120, 122, *123*
  conceptual model for, 125–126, *125*
  conceptualization of study on, 120
  demographic differences in, 123, *124*, 125
  experience indicators, 126
  further research on, 127
  implication of study on, 127
  methodology of study on, 120, *121*
  overview of, 117, 119
  phone credit and, 122–123, *124*
  products purchased and, 122–123, *124*
  pros and cons of, 126
  reliability in study on, 120, *121*, 122–123, *123*
  trust and, 120, *123*, 125–127, *125*
  validity in study on, 120, 122–123, *123*
Model comparison, 81, *82–83*, 84
Moriyoshi, Naoko, 24, 117–118
Motivated forgetting, 23, 25–27

Multi-item scales, 131
Myung-Bak, Lee, 66

Nation competency, 70, *71*, 77, 78–79, 80–81, *82–83*, 84–85, *84*
Nation equity
  consumer decision making and, 68
  defining, 63, 67
  exports and, 70, *71*
  questions about, 68, 85
  studies
    consumer preferences and, 67–68
    data collection in, 69–70, *70*, *71*, *72*
    discussion of, 84–85
    models for estimating consumer demand and, 70, 72
    moderating effects and, 72–77, 84
    relative nation brand index and, 72
    results of, empirical, 77, *78–79*, 80–81, *82–83*, 84, *84*
    Thai consumer preferences and, 63–64, 68–70, *70*, *71*, 72–77, *72*, *78–79*, 80–81, *82–83*, 84–85, *84*
National brand indexes (NBI), 67, 70
Nested logit model, 68, 75–77, *78–79*, 81, *82–83*, 84
"Neuro-culture" interaction, 14
Ng, Andy, 46
Nysveen, H., 120

OECD (Organization for Economic Cooperation and Development) study (2010), 4
Oltman, P.K., 30
One-child policy in China, 6
Online behavior of Eastern vs. Western users, 117, 129–132
Orthogonal design matrix, 69
Out-group price fairness, 15
Ownership experiences, 23, 29–32

Paradox of possessions, 23, 29–32
Pecotich, A., 68
Pedersen, P.E., 120
Penz, Elfriede, 64
People as dimension of nation competency, 70, *71*
PepsiCo Americas Beverages, 139
Peterlik, Ria Ursula, 100
Pew Research Center study, 120, 122
Pham, Michel, 7
Planning and goal-directed behavior, 23–24, 33–37, *36*, *37*, *38*
Possession, paradox of, 23, 29–32
Practical issues
  corporate visual identities and Japanese consumers, 117–118, 139–150
  logo shape designs, 117, 135–137
  mobile phone marketing in Indonesia, 117, 119–127
  overview of, 117–118, 151
  social media usage of Eastern vs. Western users, 117, 129–132
Predictive validity, 81, 84, *84*
Prevention-focused goals, 10, 35–37, *36*, *37*, *38*
Price information and fairness, 11, 15
Price premiums or discounts, 67
Price-quality relationship, 67
Products
  counterfeit, 46, 55–58
  country-of-origin effects and, 63, 66–68, 90
  evaluation of, 46, 55–58, 61–62, 66
  "ghost-shift," 46, 56–58
  perception of, 11
  price-quality relationship and, 67
  replica, "pure," 46, 56–58
Promotion-focused goals, 10, 35–37, *36*, *37*, *38*
Purwanegara, Mustika, 117

Quay, Danny, 3

Regression analysis of consumer survey data, 63–64
Regulatory fit theory, 23–24, 34, 36–37, *36*, *37*, *38*
Relative nation brand index, 72
Reliability, 105
Replica products, "pure," 46, 56–58
Research themes on Asian consumers, emerging
  affective experiences, 16–18
  consumer psychology and, understanding, 18–19
  cultural values, beliefs and meanings, 14–16
  overview of, 9
  self-construal impact on marketing mix, 10–14
Risk-taking behavior, 45, 47–50
Ritchie, R.J.B., 59
Rohm, A.J., 120
Rokeach, M., 103–104
Rosa, José Antonio, 23
Rosenthal, M.J., 68
Russell, G., 77

Sasaki, Miho, 117–118
Saudi Arabia, 66
"Saving face" social value, 14–15
Schmitt, Bernd, 7
Schooler, R., 67
Segmentation, husband-wife, 100
Self-affirmation, 48
Self-brand connection
  of Asian consumers, 94–95
  brand episode and, 91–94
  consumer life and, 93–94
  culture-of-brand-origin and, 89–90
  defining, 89
  formation of, at early age, 91–93
  global brands and culture and, 90–91
  in globalized markets, 89
  overview of, 64
Self-construal impact on marketing mix, 10–14
Self-esteem, 45, 47–50

Self-perception, 60
"Seven Sins of Consumer Psychology," 7
Singapore conference on Asian consumers (2012), 7
Singapore-U.S. social values
  changes in, cross-sectional studies of, 105–110, *106*, *107*, *108*, *109*, *110*, *111*, 112–113, *112*
  geographic marketing and, 104
  List of Values and, 105, *106*
  monitoring, 104
  overview of, 64
  in Singapore, 108–110, *108*, *109*, *110*, *111*, 112
  temporal stability and, 104
  trends in, 110, *111*, 112–113, *112*
  understanding, importance of, 113
  in United States, 107, *107*
Situational attributions of behaviors, 60
Social identity-linked promotions, 23, 25–26
Social identity threat, 26–27
Social media usage of Eastern vs. Western users, 117, 129–132
Social values. *See also* Singapore-U.S. social values
  consumer decision making and, 103–104
  defining, 103–104
  independence vs. interdependence, 51–54
  "saving face," 14–15
  understanding, importance of, 113
Society of Consumer Psychology (SCP), 7
South Korea. *See also* South Korean brand connections
  indigenization of foreign cultures in, fear of, 66
  Korean wave and, 66, 85
  nation competency, 70, *71*, 77, *78–79*, 80–81, *82–83*, 84–85, *84*
  plastic surgery trends in, 6

South Korean brand connections
  brand episode and, 91–94
  consumer life and, 93–94
  culture-of-brand-origin and, 91–93
  formation of, at early age, 91–93
  global brands and culture, 90–91
  overview of, 64
Spanjol, Jelena, 23
Stamatogiannakis, Antonios, 45–46
Starbucks logo changes, 146–147, *148, 149*
Substitution effect, 34–35
Sultan, F., 120
Surprise gifts and Asian consumers, 17–18

Tam, Leona, 23
Tambyah, Siok Kuan, 64
Tan, Soo Jiuan, 64
Teerakapibal, Surat, 63–64
Thai consumer preference
  cultural liberty and, 65–69
  heterogeneity in, 68–69, 74–75
  indigenization of foreign cultures in, fear of, 65–66
  malleability of, 68–69
  moderating effects and, 72–77, 84
  nation equity and, 63–64, 68–70, *70, 71,* 72–77, *72, 78–79,* 80–81, *82–84,* 84–85
  overview of, 63–64
  sociodemographic variables moderating, 72–77
Thai nation competency, 70, *71,* 77, *78–79,* 80–81, *82–83,* 84–85, *84*
Theoretical issues. *See also* Research themes on Asian consumers
  "eighth sin" of consumer psychology, 7
  general theories, 5–7
  impulsive behavior and decision making, 24, 41–44

Theoretical issues *(continued)*
  motivated forgetting, 23, 25–27
  overview of, 23–24, 151
  paradox of possessions, 23, 29–32
  planning and goal-directed behavior, 23–24, 33–37, *36, 37, 38*
  "Seven Sins of Consumer Psychology," 7
Threat to social identity, 26–27
Tourism as dimension of nation competency, 70, *71*
Tropicana Pure Premium Orange Juice logo changes, 139
Trust
  deceptive advertising and, 59–62
  mobile phone marketing in Indonesia and, 120, *123,* 125–127, *125*
TV set possessions, 30–32

Uncertainty, dealing with, 45, 47–50
UNESCO report (2002), 65
United States nation competency, 70, *71, 77, 78–79,* 80–81, *82–83,* 84–85, *84. See also* Singapore-U.S. social values
Uskul, Ayse, 14

Valenzuela, Ana, 45
Validity, 81, 84, *84,* 105
Van der Lans, R., 140
Vietnamese household economic decision making, 64, 97–100

Western brands, 16
Western medicine, Asian consumers' beliefs about, 16
Whiteside, S.P., 41
Witkin, H.A., 30
World Bank report (2003), 65
Wyer, R.S., Jr., 67

Yang, Haiyang, 23, 45–46

About the Editors and Contributors

Editors

Bernd Schmitt is the Robert D. Calkins Professor of International Business at Columbia Business School. During the completion of this book he lived in Singapore, where he was the inaugural executive director of the new Institute on Asian Consumer Insight and is also Nanyang Visiting Professor at Nanyang Technological University. Dr. Schmitt is widely published and has been active as a researcher, professor, and consultant in Asia for more than twenty years.

Leonard Lee is an associate professor of marketing at the National University of Singapore Business School and was previously an associate professor of marketing at Columbia Business School. His research focuses on investigating why and how consumers shop in real-world environments and how experiential and environmental factors affect their shopping behavior. He is also interested in understanding how emotional and cognitive factors influence consumer judgments and decision-making. His research has been published in major academic journals and featured in popular media such as the *New York Times*, *Financial Times*, and the *Wall Street Journal*.

Contributors

Nelson Amaral is an assistant professor of marketing at the Kogod School of Business, American University.

Donnel Briley is professor of marketing at the University of Sydney.

Ziv Carmon is the INSEAD Chaired Professor of Marketing in Memory of Erin Anderson at INSEAD, Singapore.

Steven Chan is an assistant professor of marketing at the Sy Syms School of Business, Yeshiva University.

Amitava Chattopadhyay is the INSEAD Chaired Professor of Marketing and Creativity at INSEAD, Singapore, and a Fellow of the Institute on Asian Consumer Insight.

Sunmyoung Cho is a senior researcher of the Symbiotic Life-TECH at the Yonsei University in Seoul, South Korea.

Amy N. Dalton is a faculty member in the Department of Marketing at the Hong Kong University of Science and Technology.

Peter Darke is Full Professor, Department of Marketing, Schulich School of Business, York University in Toronto, Canada.

Ravi Dhar is the George Rogers Clark Professor of Management and Marketing at Yale University.

Maria Galli is an assistant professor of marketing at Universitat Pompeu Fabra, Barcelona, Spain.

Gerald J. Gorn is a chair professor of marketing at the Hong Kong Polytechnic University.

Li Huang is a doctoral student in marketing at the University of South Carolina.

Mia Tantri Diah Indriani (MSc) is a lecturer at Management from School of Business and Management, Bandung Institute of Technology (ITB), Indonesia.

Yuwei Jiang is an assistant professor of marketing at the Hong Kong Polytechnic University.

Pavitra Jindahra is a faculty of marketing at Sasin Graduate of School Business Administration, Chulalongkorn University, Bangkok, Thailand.

Lynn R. Kahle is the Ehrman Giustina Professor and Head of the Department of Marketing at the University of Oregon, where he is also the Thomas Cook Distinguished Professor.

Erich Kirchler is on the faculty of psychology at the University of Vienna.

Werner H. Kunz is assistant professor of marketing at the University of Massachusetts Boston.

Raymond R. Liu is associate professor of marketing at the College of Management, University of Massachusetts Boston.

Naoko Moriyoshi is an associate professor Faculty of Business and Commerce, Keio University, Japan.

Andy H. Ng is a PhD candidate in social psychology at York University.

Michael Nicholson is Director of the Global Learning Centre and Executive Education at Durham University Business School, Durham, UK.

Elfriede Penz is at the Vienna University of Economics and Business (WU Vienna), Institute for International Marketing Management.

Ronny Armando Pitojo received a bachelor's degree in management from School of Business and Management, Bandung Institute of Technology (ITB), Indonesia.

Mustika Sufiati Purwanegara is an associate professor in the School of Business and Management, Bandung Institute of Technology (ITB), Indonesia.

José Antonio Rosa is a professor of marketing and sustainable business practices at the University of Wyoming.

Miho Sasaki is Associate Professor, Faculty of Business and Commerce, Keio University, Japan.

Jelena Spanjol is an associate professor of marketing at the University of Illinois at Chicago.

Antonios Stamatogiannakis is an assistant professor of marketing at IE Business School—IE University, Madrid, Spain.

Leona Tam is an associate professor of marketing at the University of Wollongong in Australia.

Siok Kuan Tambyah is a senior lecturer at the National University of Singapore.

Soo Jiuan Tan is an associate professor in the department of marketing at the National University of Singapore.

Surat Teerakapibal is a PhD candidate in marketing at the Sasin Graduate of School Business Administration, Chulalongkorn University, Bangkok, Thailand.

Ana Valenzuela is associate professor of marketing at Baruch College, CUNY, and visiting professor at the Barcelona School of Management, Universitat Pompeu Fabra, Barcelona, Spain.

Sarah Hong Xiao is a lecturer in marketing at the University of Durham, Durham, UK.

Haiyang Yang is an assistant professor of marketing at the Johns Hopkins University, Baltimore.

CPSIA information can be obtained at www.ICGtesting.com
Printed in the USA
BVOW06s1321030915

416466BV00009B/84/P